THE RULES™ FOR MARRIAGE

Time-tested Secrets for
Making Your Marriage Work

ELLEN FEIN
AND SHERRIE SCHNEIDER

Warner Books, Inc., 1271 Avenue of the Americas, New York, NY 10020

Visit our Web site at www.twbookmark.com

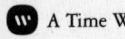 A Time Warner Company

Printed in the United States of America

First Printing: June 2001
10 9 8 7 6 5 4 3 2 1

Library of Congress Cataloging-in-Publication Data

Fein, Ellen.
    The rules for marriage : time-tested secrets for making your marriage work /
Ellen Fein and Sherrie Schneider.
        p. cm.
    ISBN: 0-446-52696-7
    1. Marriage.   2. Interpersonal relations.   I. Schneider, Sherrie.   II. Title.

HQ734 F367 2001
306.81—dc21   00-051338

Book design by Giorgetta Bell McRee

Contents

THE RULES FOR MARRIAGE

Foreword _____

Why We Wrote
The Rules for Marriage

Have you ever wondered why some women are happily married while others are not, why some are content and others are constantly fighting with their spouses and feeling miserable? The truth is, marriage isn't easy. If it were, 50 percent of marriages wouldn't end in divorce. Why are some marriages less successful than others? Success takes work. You might not want to hear this, but no one wanted to believe you had to work to get a man to propose either—before *The Rules*—and let's face it, you do. So if you are willing to work hard to get a man, we think you'll agree it's worth some effort to keep him. That's why we came up with *The Rules for Marriage*.

Do these rules apply to you? Well, do any of these problems sound familiar?

"When we were dating, we did interesting things all the time. Now that we're married, his idea of fun is sitting on the couch, eating potato chips and watching TV."

"I want children now. He wants to wait a few years."

"His ex-girlfriend still calls every once in a while and sends him birthday cards. How do I deal with this?"

"I like sex in the morning, he likes it at night."

"I love him, but not his parents."

"I resent the fact that I make more money than he does; I think he resents it, too."

These are problems many of our readers shared with us so we've done a great deal of research on how to solve them—in some cases, by avoiding them in the first place. *The Rules for Marriage* gives you answers to these problems and more.

When we wrote *The Rules* in 1995, we studied what worked and didn't work in dating. We noticed that women who acted "hard to get" got their man, while women who were too available or eager got hurt. We compiled thirty-five rules that helped women to be more of a challenge to men, such as "don't talk to a man first" and "end the date first." As difficult as these rules were to do, they had to be followed strictly only for the first three or four months of the relationship. In many cases, it was best to do them until the man proposed—but after that time, you know he's committed, so you can relax a bit.

Marriage, on the other hand, is long-term. So *The Rules for Marriage,* while certainly not as strict as *The Rules* for dating, must be a way of life. *The Rules* for dating are like a short-term diet—you don't have sex with him and act mysterious for a few months to make him fall in love with you in the same way that you don't eat dessert for a few months so you can fit into your bathing suit for the summer. The *Rules for Marriage,* however, are like a lifelong maintenance plan. Anybody can lose twenty pounds, but how many keep it off? Lots of women know how to catch a man, but how many stay happily married? Our focus here is not on getting a man, but keeping him. This means doing what it takes to make him happy. This can be as basic as making him feel important, being considerate, a team player, and it can also mean doing a bit extra—making a conscious effort not to nag, or to be supportive of his ideas. All of this requires *work*.

Unfortunately and whether you accept it or not, most or all of the emotional work in a marriage must be done by *you*. It is not mutual. Proof: *You* are reading this book, not your husband. He is probably reading a thriller or a book about making more money in the stock market. We are not generalizing. This is just the way it is. In fact, your husband may not even like the fact that you are reading this book or talking to your friends or mother about your marital problems. Like most men, he does not like to talk to outsiders about his private life and believes that you should be able to solve your problems yourself or with him. So we don't recommend discussing this book with your husband, or asking him to read it. Even if he agrees with most or all of our advice, he doesn't like to think that you have to read a book to learn how to deal with him.

Maybe your husband is different. Maybe you have one of those rare husbands who reads relationship books and puts a lot of thought into keeping your relationship strong. We salute you—and him—but most women don't have that kind of husband and we are writing to most women.

The fact is, to be happily married, a woman sometimes needs to treat her husband like a client or customer whom she wants to keep happy (let him be right). You're probably thinking, "Why can't it be equal? Why doesn't *he* have to do all the things you're suggesting, like don't say the first mean word or make up first?" Our answer: because that's the way it is. Men and women are different. They're different when they're dating—the man must be the pursuer—and they're different when they're married—the woman must do most of the emotional work in a relationship. We didn't make this up—in fact, we would love to give you different advice, but these ideas are based on human nature, and like it or not, they work. So don't count on your husband doing his "part;" he may or may not. But he will respond in kind if you do yours. He will be happy and want to stay with you forever. As one newly married businesswoman who consulted with us for marital advice said, "Men require so much work. Every woman has to work in a relationship with a man. Nothing is wrong with a woman if she needs these *Rules for Marriage.* Some women know a bit more about how to do it than others, but all of us need reminding."

So we present to you *The Rules for Marriage.* You will find some rules harder than others, you won't be perfect and you will make mistakes. The important thing is to make a beginning and keep trying. In no time, you will *want* to do *The Rules for Marriage* for no other reason than because they really work! Good luck!

Ellen and Sherrie

Note: Between the writing of this book and its publication, Ellen has separated from her husband. The lessons learned in working on this book have taught her the true value of a *Rules* marriage, and she is more committed to *The Rules* than ever. She thanks her readers for their support.

Rule #1:

Relax During the Engagement and Wedding

Ideally, *The Rules for Marriage* begin before your wedding day. We believe once you get engaged, a wedding date should be set—no endless engagements. When a man proposes, it should be with a ring and a wedding date within one year, not longer, unless you are young (under twenty-five years old), in which case a two-year engagement is fine. If your fiancé is stalling on a wedding date, you may have to give him back the ring and move on.

Assuming you have a ring and a reasonable wedding date, what are the rules for the engagement period and wedding?

Every month we receive calls, letters, and e-mail saying, "Thanks. I'm so happy!" But we also get letters like this one: "Now that I'm engaged, we're fighting all the time. I feel him pulling back. I'm acting needy. What should I do?" Or like this one: "How often should I see him now that I'm engaged? Do I stick to the three-day-a-week rule and ten-minute phone calls?"

These concerns are fairly common. The dynamics of a relationship can change dramatically when you go from dating to being engaged and planning the wedding. It is tempting to change your behavior—to call him all the time, to lose interest in yourself, your work, your friends, and just about everything else—because, after all, you are practically married. All of a sudden, you think *The Rules* are over. This is a mistake. A man may get overwhelmed if he suddenly sees and/or hears from you morning, noon, and night. It's not like he's going to break the engagement, but he starts to miss his freedom and wants space (going out with the guys, working late) and then you get hurt.

If you continue to do *The Rules,* this will not happen. We don't recommend living together, as we said in *The Rules,* but if you are and you are planning the wedding, continue to be "a creature unlike any other" (confident, easygoing), remain focused on making your life full and meaningful, and try not to nag him about the wedding plans or anything else.

However, the initial rigid rules of catching a husband no longer apply now. He already pursued you, told you he loves you, and wants to marry you. You're a couple now, so you can relax in the knowledge that you don't need to stick to the original "don't see him more than three times a week or talk for more than ten minutes on the phone" rules. You will be seeing him more often since you are planning the wedding and your future or even living together. Obviously, you will need to call him to discuss things. The key here is *how* you conduct yourself—you're calm, fun, pleasant, you still have your own life, you're not suddenly demanding or clingy—that will make all the difference between a happy engagement and a stressful one. You don't have to be a constant challenge. He enjoys just being with you. Also, you can call him at work more often than when you were dating. Just try to make sure the calls are quick and to the point, not an excuse to speak to him or to have marathon discussions. A sample conversation about the wedding: "Hi hon, the flowers are in, my fitting is Tuesday, talk to you later, love you. . . ."

Now, about the wedding planning: Most women can get pretty hysterical while planning their wedding—there are *so* many details to worry about, so many pressures for it to go smoothly, so many opinions from family, friends, and relatives. Try to keep your sanity. If you act like a diva or a perfectionist, you will make everyone around you crazy, including your fiancé. Relax! This is a good time to go inward, to not let Hollywood images of a perfect wedding distract you from the meaning of it all. You will soon be marrying the man of your dreams. Try to remember that the wedding is just one day of your life, not a motion-picture production. So what if the flowers are more lilac than pink? So what if the photographer you really wanted is booked and you have to go with your second choice? Are you going to let all this ruin your big day? This is a good time to take up yoga or meditation so you keep your priorities straight.

We all know women who made themselves nervous wrecks over their wedding plans and hardly even enjoyed their big day. Of course, they all regretted it. Don't let this happen to you. Don't let family and friends make you crazy about the seating arrangements. Don't lose sleep worrying if the buffet is big enough, if guests are going to starve or complain about the food. Nobody's ever starved at a wedding and what people think of the buffet is not that important. There will always be critics who think that there could have been more hot dishes or that the band was too loud. Do the best you can. You can't please everyone. This is a valuable lesson to learn as you plan the wedding, and it will come in handy when you are married, too. Do your best and then let it go! Make yourself happy and others will follow your lead.

How involved your fiancé is in the wedding plans is also not something you can or should try to control. Some men refuse to be left out of anything. This type will not be satisfied with interviewing one or two caterers or bands or photographers, he will want to see the half dozen who are the cream of the crop. He will agonize over picking the perfect wedding song and even take an interest in the floral arrangements. He wants it to be a once-in-a-lifetime experience because he doesn't plan to get married again. He will be the same about the honeymoon, calling the best hotels for the honeymoon suites (which could probably accommodate a party of six) on a high floor with elegant views of the city. He will make dinner reservations for the most intimate corner tables at the finest restaurants. Money will be no object, even if he doesn't have much. Be thrilled if your fiancé shows this much interest. Go along with his enthusiasm even if you're not as into it as he is. Some brides are not as fortunate.

Your fiancé may show little or no interest in wedding plans; he thinks it's a woman's thing and would go along with "whatever"—he'd be just as happy to exchange vows with both your immediate families, a few close friends, and a vase of flowers in his one-bedroom apartment. Do not force him to get involved. Don't analyze his indifference or nag him to take a more active role, just accept that some men are simply not interested in the intricacies of a wedding, even their own. They will show up at the altar, but that's about it. If this is the case, plan the wedding with your bridesmaids, family, and friends, and be glad that he has confidence in your planning abilities.

As for disagreements, try to take them in stride. Suppose you and your fiancé have different ideas about the size of the wedding. You want a big affair, he wants a small one. You want a band, he wants a D.J. You want to hire a professional photographer, he wants to ask his friend Joe to take snapshots—you get the idea! Don't throw tantrums, act like a diva, or insist on having your way. Maybe a small wedding isn't such a bad idea, especially if he's trying to save money to buy a house and start a family. Whatever his reasons, we think it's important to listen and consider his point of view. Don't impose your fairy-tale images of a lavish Cinderella wedding on him. Cut him some slack—he pursued you, proposed, bought you a ring, and has made a commitment to spend the rest of his life with you. If you demand a big, expensive wedding and he's not into it, neither of you will be happy. Besides, bickering a lot before the wedding is not a fun way to walk down the aisle!

The most enjoyable weddings are the ones where the bride and groom are happy and in love, so if you have that going for you, your wedding will be all you want it to be.

Rule #2:

Continue to Be a Creature Unlike Any Other (a CUAO)

When you were single, being a "creature unlike any other" was all about attitude—having the self-confidence to weather a bad date and holding on to the conviction that you would one day find the right man, the man who would love you for the unique person you are. We asked you to pump yourself up before dates, and believe in yourself.

When you're married, you must continue to believe that you are a creature unlike any other, but now it means having confidence that your husband loves and appreciates you, and that you can have a successful and fulfilling marriage. In other words, apply the self-confidence you had while dating to being a happily married woman. Exactly what do we mean? Here are some examples:

Maintain a positive attitude. It helps to be optimistic, not cynical—and to look at the glass as half full. You still believe in love and marriage, even if some of your friends are divorced or this is *your* second marriage. You smile a lot. You're easy to be with. You're not a grievance collector. You don't hold grudges because you know that grudges hurt *you* more than the other person and add wrinkles and years to your life, so you don't tolerate them for more than five minutes. You believe that good things happen to good people most of the time, so you try to be good. You don't care if people think you are naive or a Pollyanna. It makes you happy to think this way, and that's what counts.

If you work, you do your work and go home. You don't make work your whole life. You are balanced. You believe in family first, business second. Your priorities are straight, and you're not jealous of what other people have or do.

Don't make mountains out of molehills. For example, if you trust your husband and he talks to an attractive woman at a party, you don't spend the entire car ride home grilling him about her. "So did you think she was pretty? If you were single, would you have asked her out?" Leave him alone. Your husband is allowed to talk to another woman or find her attractive. It just means he's a man and has eyes. Sometimes a married woman will call us to complain that her husband's ex-girlfriend calls once a year just to say hello. She wants to know how she should handle this. We tell her to do nothing. As long as *her* husband is not the one calling the ex, there's no problem.

You're in control, and you make an effort to be calm. Whether you practice yoga or meditation, the 12 Steps, light candles, read the Bible, or go to temple on Saturday or church on Sunday, try to figure out some way to rise above the daily craziness of life, the trivialities, and the petty annoyances that can bog down a marriage. Stay centered, know that the daily discipline of exercise or prayer or whatever it is you do will give you the strength to get through everything so you set aside the time to take care of yourself in this way. Hence, you don't live from crisis to crisis. Your life is not a soap opera. You don't let people or events ruin your serenity. You know that happiness comes from within.

But you're not an evangelist. If you are into some self-improvement program, are anti-fur, a vegetarian, an ex-smoker, or "born again," you are not trying to convert everyone you come into contact with. (Nobody likes a zealot. They're boring.) You know that you just have to live your life and not try to change anyone. You believe in live and let live—beginning with your husband and your children—and you are serene.

In the rest of this book, you will find more than forty ways to help you continue to be a "creature unlike any other" throughout your marriage.

Rule #3:

Keep Up Your Looks—
But Don't Go Crazy

Let's be realistic, a good marriage is based on a lot more than looks. Your husband obviously found you attractive or he wouldn't have married you in the first place, so don't think you have to look like a movie star every day or save money for plastic surgery to keep him. Nips and tucks don't make husbands happy or keep them around. And truth be told, a lot of men find those long nail extensions scary and useless—they wonder how you could possibly change a diaper or type on the computer without breaking them.

On the other hand, just because you are married does not mean that you should let yourself go. Strive for something in between glam and drab, like well-groomed and pretty. Remember how we told you to wear short skirts and get weekly manicures when you were dating? Well, now that you're married, you can relax a little! Your husband is not looking for a perfectly coiffed salon advertisement, but a warm, loving partner. So don't think you have to pore over the latest fashion magazines to be absolutely current and in style. It's perfectly okay to hang out in a T-shirt, shorts, and sandals with your hair in a ponytail—everyone we know does!

Now that you're married, it's more important that you maintain composure and are organized about your home, your life, your kids, your work. A spritz of perfume before he comes home goes a long way toward maintaining your sex appeal, and shows him you still care, without going overboard.

You're neat, clean, responsible, loving, and nice—that's sexy. You're not trying to compete with his twenty-five-year-old secretary. You don't have to wear fake eyelashes or live in a beauty salon. Two coats of mascara and short, clean nails are fine. No need to look into liposuction or breast implants. Maybe you have five or ten pounds to lose? That's okay too. Your husband is not looking for a mannequin. He would rather you be nice than a supermodel.

However, don't pack on thirty pounds after the wedding or make it a habit to walk around the house in oversize pajamas and dirty hair. Take care of yourself. Try to exercise two to three times a week, to maintain your equilibrium, shape, and energy level, and try to wear clothes that flatter your figure.

Wear your hair long even though it's easier to wear it short and most of your married friends have cut their hair to the middle of their neck. Long hair reminds you that you're a woman, and your husband probably likes it long and you want to please him. Don't walk around with dark roots; touch up any gray in your hair. You believe in helping Mother Nature. Brush your hair and put on a dab of makeup before leaving the house even to go to the supermarket. Remember, if you feel good about your appearance, you will look good, so you are doing this for yourself!

Rule #4: ─────────────────

Keep Up Your Own Interests (Have a Life!)

Some women make their husbands their whole life when they get married and drop many of the things that made them interesting in the first place. Some lose interest in their careers or stop working altogether. Some see less of their family and friends, and others cut back on interests and activities, including exercise. This is a mistake that we would like to help you avoid. We have encountered many women who became half a person in their marriage and came to regret it later.

Right after Amy married Phil, she quit her job as a real-estate agent to concentrate on getting pregnant, learning how to cook, and decorating their house. She also dropped some of her single friends. For years, she had met five girlfriends every Wednesday night for dinner and a movie ("girls night out") but decided to skip it so she could eat dinner and watch TV with her husband. Phil didn't discourage it. In fact, he seemed flattered that she preferred his company and was happy when Amy told him she couldn't relate to her single friends anymore. But after a few months, Phil started to tire of so much togetherness. When he came home he wanted to read a book (alone) instead of watch TV with Amy. He started making plans with the guys once a week to shoot hoops or go out for drinks.

Amy was hurt and angry. She had dropped her friends to spend every evening with Phil and now he was bored with her. Realizing the mistake she made, she went back to girls night out and took a part-time job. Amy learned a painful but important lesson.

Many men will be flattered or even encourage their wives to drop friends or activities for them, only to lose interest in them when they do. Despite what they say, men like women the most when they're busy. They love coming home to women who lead exciting lives, who are busy exercising or writing a novel on their computer, who will tell them an interesting story about some friends or a coworker, or who have to dash because they don't want to miss their yoga class. They like it when you've got other things going on besides them and have to fight a little for your attention.

Have you ever noticed that your husband wants to talk to you the most when you're on the phone or in the middle of something, as opposed to when you're eager to talk or just sitting around doing nothing or waiting for him to come home? If you listen to what a man thinks he wants and make him your whole life, he will get bored and pull back and you will feel hurt and regret it.

"Husbands get bored when women only concentrate on them," says Nancy, who made that very mistake in her first year of marriage. She got busy in the second year by getting a job and taking ballet twice a week. "The more stuff I do, the more interested he is in me. I feel better about myself and my personality is more interesting, so he's more attracted to me and now when we're together he really appreciates me," she said. "You need to have a life apart from your husband."

Andrea, a former book editor and now a stay-at-home mom who has been happily married for five years, concurs. "I have activities and friends apart from my husband. I have been on a tennis team for four years and we practice and play twice a week all year round. I also belong to a monthly book club. I have taken classes at a local college and I have participated in different church functions. I think married women must have outlets away from their home or else there's too much strain on the husband-wife relationship. And I must say it is nice to see how much my husband misses me when I spend a Sunday afternoon playing tennis. Sometimes he even comes to watch me play without my asking him to. He says he doesn't want to be away from me too long."

Of course, another reason to have a life when you are married is that you will be less likely to break *Rules*. Women who are bored and restless are most likely to call their husbands a lot at work, nag, complain, find fault with them, or try to change them because they have too much time on their hands or are not happy with themselves. When you are involved in something, be it an interesting career, meeting friends for dinner and a movie, exercising, taking night courses, or doing charity work, you are busy, focused on yourself, and less likely to bother your husband. Maybe you can't relate to Amy because her case is so extreme, but here is a more common scenario:

While Joan didn't make Tom her whole life, she found it hard to put herself first at times and got hurt. When she was single, she loved to take exercise classes early Sunday morning, her only day off from her retail clothing business. Tom thought it would be nice to spend Sunday mornings in bed together, eating breakfast and reading the newspaper. She agreed that it would be romantic too, so she stopped going to her favorite 9 A.M. class. After a few months, Tom started to sleep late on Sundays—sometimes until noon. An early riser, Joan would putter around the house for hours waiting for Tom to wake up. She finally asked him one Sunday, "What happened to breakfast in bed? I've been up for hours." Tom said work was exhausting and he needed to catch up on his sleep. "Why don't you go to the gym?" he asked. Joan was furious. When she was running off to the gym, he wanted to do things together. Now that she was around, he wanted to sleep late!

When a man turns the tables on you like that, it's easy to feel like a victim and make a big issue out of it. Don't! He's just human. We don't always know what *we* want either! You're better off resuming your activities and dropping the subject. Just realize that men are used to taking care of themselves, they don't have to read books on codependence, they naturally put themselves first. Women, on the other hand, tend to be caretakers, wanting to please everyone else and putting themselves last, and then feeling like victims when they're not appreciated. It's important to find a happy medium. You should not be so busy that you have no time for your husband, but there is no reason you can't pursue your career, see your girlfriends once a week, or take exercise classes and still have time for him. Your husband should be the most important person in your life, but he should not be everything or nothing. Strive for balance. Regardless of what he thinks or says, he will be happier when you are fulfilled and busy.

But the reason you need to remain interesting is for you, not him. Why stop growing as a person just because you are married? We know women who read the newspaper religiously and followed politics with fascination when they were single, but once they were married they totally lost touch with current events. You should not become brain-dead just because you are married.

Mindy's problem was a little different, but you can probably relate. She didn't want to make a decision without her husband's input. When she was single she was very decisive. She ran an executive-recruitment firm, decorated her own apartment by herself, and traveled the world alone. But after being married a few months, she lost her initiative. She didn't want to think for herself. When she felt the kitchen floor needed retiling, she wanted Andy to help her pick the colors. When she had to choose drapes for the living room, she wanted Andy, a CPA, to go with her to look at fabrics, during the middle of tax season.

"I just can't take off anytime. Figure it out yourself, or go with your mother. Whatever you decide is fine with me. Really!" Andy told her. Mindy was so afraid of making a mistake that she wanted to put off decorating until after tax season. She would rather sit in a half-furnished house for six months than make a decision. It wasn't bad for Mindy to ask her husband's opinion, but once it was clear he wasn't interested, she should have persevered on her own.

This kind of fear and codependence is quite common among married women. If you're anything like Mindy, you need to be told that being married doesn't mean being joined at the hip, that all decisions don't have to be made with your husband especially when he shows no interest, that if you keep doing nothing while waiting for your husband's approval you will have no backbone or self-esteem, and that it's okay to make mistakes. Women like Mindy sometimes need to "act single"—just go out and buy the tiles—or nothing will get done.

Being happily married means finding a balance of togetherness and independence. Women who stop living their lives or depend too much on their husbands for companionship or decision-making end up feeling unhappy and unfulfilled and their husbands know it. Don't let this happen to you!

Rule #5:

Lower Your Expectations in the First Year

For some couples, the first year of marriage is a continuation of the honeymoon. For others, it can be quite an adjustment period. He wants things his way, you want things your way, and you can't believe he won't change for you. If he really loved you, he would change, right? Welcome to the first year of marriage where arguments about where to live, how often to see your family, how to spend money, what to have for dinner, and so on can take their toll on a relationship.

Unfortunately, sometimes there is no answer to your differences, no right or wrong. And very often, it's just the little things that set you off. For example, you want the air-conditioning off, he likes it on all the time and tells you on a hot summer day, "Why don't you wear a sweater if you're cold?" Meanwhile, you think he should see a specialist about his snoring. He thinks you're overreacting and accuses you of being a light sleeper. You like to watch movies in utter silence as if you were all by yourself. He likes to watch movies as a couple, explaining the plot as it unfolds and commenting on the actors ("She looks familiar . . . wasn't she in . . . ?"), causing you to miss bits and pieces of dialogue. You tell him to be quiet, he gets offended, and you feel guilty, and now this little friction makes you miss bits and pieces of the movie. You envision your apartment with a minimalist look—black leather couches, white Formica furniture, a couple of nice modern paintings, and silver artwork on the mantel above the fireplace. He wants to put his fifteen-year-old plaid recliner with the stuffing coming out of it in the living room, a gaudy bronze baseball trophy he won in college on the fireplace, and antique family heirlooms on the coffee table. You can't believe you married someone with such bad taste and tell him so. He gets angry and sulks in his broken recliner. In your worst nightmare, you never imagined that your first year of marriage would be about *this!*

Relax. Most first-year marriage differences can be solved simply by lowering your expectations. Don't expect to see eye-to-eye on everything. Just because you love each other doesn't mean you're going to think and feel the same way about everything. Some of the most happily married couples don't! So don't compare your marriage to TV movies and Hallmark cards showing marital bliss or to your friend's "perfect" marriage. The movies are not real and your friend's marriage is not perfect. In some cases, just agreeing to disagree can take the edge off; in others, somebody has to adjust and see the other person's point of view. In those cases, why not give it a try?

Here are some true first-year marriage stories and the

advice we gave the wives. Perhaps you can relate and apply the answers to your own situation.

Bait and switch is a very common first-year problem. Your husband behaved one way when you were dating and now he behaves another way. For example, Don was incredibly generous with money when he was dating Peggy. Fine restaurants, flowers, lavish gifts, and expensive trips were commonplace. But when they got married, Santa Claus turned into Scrooge. He wanted to eat only in Chinese restaurants, scrutinized Peggy's credit card charges, and talked constantly about investments. Most of their fights had to do with Peggy's spending. One of the worst was when she came home one cold Saturday afternoon in January and took off her socks and shoes to relax. Don noticed that she had gotten a pedicure and blurted out: "Why do you need a pedicure in the winter? Who's going to see your toes? You're wasting money. Why can't you do it yourself?" A two-hour argument ensued.

"The pedicure cost $15 and *I'm* going to see my toes in the winter. You spent $15 on appetizers when we were dating. Why are you making this a federal case?" She then launched into a twenty-minute speech about how she works just as hard as he does and is entitled to some pampering. Don wanted to know how they were going to save for a house and kids if Peggy threw away money on salons, long-distance phone calls to friends around the country, and endless pairs of shoes. Peggy said, "You're overreacting, $15 isn't going to make or break a down payment," to which Don replied, "It adds up. Besides, you can't spend money like you're single anymore. We have to build a nest egg."

When Peggy contacted us, we explained that Don's behavior was not so unusual. When a man is dating, he's trying to impress you, but when he's married he's thinking of other things like paying the mortgage and saving for the kids' college tuition. Peggy needed to lower her expectations—not to expect Don to be oblivious to finances and not to feel offended if he questioned her spending. We suggested she even appreciate it that Don cared so much about their future security. We did not tell Peggy to cut back on her spending—that is her business—but to see Don's point of view and allow him to worry and make comments about money without getting defensive or self-righteous. We suggested that she think about how she spent her money, and if the expense was worth it to her, to respond rationally, not angrily, so the next time Don scrutinized her spending, she could calmly reply, "I know, you may be right, but I really like pedicures. They make me feel good."

Maybe your husband's bait and switch is that he used to want to go out a lot and have fun and now he's glued to the TV and a little boring. Perhaps your husband's change in behavior is that he ran marathons when you were dating and now he snacks constantly, let his gym membership expire, and has gained thirty pounds. In this case, there is nothing you can do but live with it. It is unrealistic to expect a man to act exactly the way he did when he was dating you. We would venture to guess that you probably don't exercise as much, wear as much makeup or those uncomfortable high heels and padded bras now that you did when you were single. The same goes for men. Once they're comfortable with you, they tend to relax in their own ways, be it spending less or eating more or not shaving. They're not trying to impress you every waking moment. Don't expect them to. Know that it will just take some time of adjustment before you both are used to each other's behavior, and have faith that it will even out after the first year.

Different schedules and habits can also wreak havoc in the first year of marriage. Here is another true story: Cindy knew Steve liked rock music when they were dating, but didn't notice until they were married that he played the stereo loudly every day when he woke up at six A.M. She didn't have to wake up for work until 7 A.M. and preferred the gentle sounds of birds chirping in their backyard. Every morning she woke up with resentment—not only was she up an hour earlier, but she had to listen to deafening music. She asked Steve if he could stop playing the music in the morning, and just listen to the radio in the car on the way to work.

"I've been waking up to music my whole life. I need it to help me get started in the morning. Why don't you wear earplugs or something?" he objected. Cindy tried earplugs but they only cut the sound in half. More upsetting than the music was Steve's refusal to compromise. If he loved her, wouldn't he care about her extra sleep and serenity? "How could I have married someone so inconsiderate?" she asked us.

We told Cindy that she couldn't expect her husband to change a lifelong habit and asked if there was anything that could turn her earlier waking time to her advantage, like going to morning sessions at a gym. She now takes a 6 A.M. aerobics class and leaves Steve alone to enjoy his music, and she is thrilled to have her workout out of the way before her workday even begins. Sometimes compromise can work to your advantage.

Theresa also had to learn to adjust, rather than insist on her fantasies about the first year of marriage. She had always assumed that newlyweds ate dinner together, at least most of the time. A schoolteacher, she was home by 4 P.M. and usually cooked a gourmet meal for her pediatrician husband Robert to eat at 6 P.M. Yet almost every evening, he called to say he would be late. First he would call to say he would be ten minutes late, then a half hour, then "go ahead, eat without me." There was either an emergency or paperwork or an errand he had to do on the way home. He would come home around 7 or 8 P.M. and she would have to reheat his meal and just watch him eat. This dining schedule was not what she had expected in her marriage.

We advised Theresa to be realistic about the nature of her husband's work. We told her to just assume she would be eating alone Monday through Friday and be pleasantly surprised if she didn't, to invite a friend over or find something to do between 6 and 8 P.M. so that she just wasn't waiting in the kitchen for Robert's call and fuming. Once she was able to accept the reality of her weeknight dining, the couple was able to make the best of the situation. They have turned their weekend dinners into special occasions, cooking together or splurging on romantic dinners out. Both of them look forward to these dinners all week.

Some first-year marriage dilemmas are more serious than eating dinner together. Here is Betty and Barry's story: Giddy in love, Betty did not think twice about leaving her friends, family, and career in the city, where she had lived her whole life, to move to the rural suburbs where Barry owned a home and business. She just assumed that love would conquer all. But by their second month of marriage, Betty realized that she could not stand the sight of deer in her backyard, missed the city, and was bored and lonely. She complained morning, noon, and night. "If you loved me, you'd move to New York," she would tell Barry. Her husband refused to relocate. "You'll get used to it, everyone does," he reassured her. She found his answers cold and callous; easy for him to say, he's lived here his whole life!

After fighting for another six months about where to live, Betty contacted us. We told her that if she wanted to stay married to Barry, she had to accept their living situation and that it was unrealistic to think he would relocate. We counseled her to stop telling Barry how unhappy she was and put her energy instead into finding work and meeting people in her area. Sentences beginning with "if you loved me" or "I hate the suburbs" should be removed from her conversation. The plan took time, but after a few months she found a part-time job in her neighborhood and made a few friends by taking a night course and joining a gym. Suddenly, the suburbs didn't seem so bad. Plus, Barry was so pleased by her adjustments that he suggested a weekend trip to New York City, and liked it so much that it became a frequent activity.

If you are sparring with your husband over a serious or petty issue, try lowering your expectations of marital bliss. You may be pleasantly surprised, for he may appreciate your compassion and respond by meeting you halfway. Remember, the only way to get your way all the time is to live by yourself—and even that is no guarantee. A noisy neighbor next to your lonely apartment can interrupt your sleep just as much as a snoring husband!

Rule #6:

Be a Team

Weтold you in *The Rules* to be independent, to keep your own life—career interests, hobbies, friends—when you meet Mr. Right. This is necessary because many women tend to drop everything and everyone when they start dating a man they really like. They become too involved, see him too often too early on, and he eventually loses interest. Like it or not, men very often fall in love with women who initially appear able to take them or leave them. And, in Rule #4, we reminded you to keep up your own interests and have a life.

But be careful to strike a balance—the same independent spirit that helped him fall in love with you and keeps him interested can backfire if you go too far in this direction. For a truly successful marriage, it is essential to remember that you are now part of a team.

While you should certainly continue to cultivate your career, friends, and interests throughout your marriage, you must retrain yourself to think as a couple, not a single person. Before you plunge into things as if you were still single, try to take his feelings and opinions into account. For example, before you make plans with a girlfriend to grab dinner and a movie—no big deal, right?—run it by him. It's not that you are asking permission, it's just that he might want to see that movie with *you,* and it might make sense to choose a different one tonight.

Little courtesies of this kind can make a big difference. For example, try to wait to have dinner together when he calls to say he'll be a half hour late, even though the food is hot, you're starving, and a little annoyed—what is half an hour compared to the enjoyment of a shared dinner?

Make sure you have at least twenty minutes together at some point during the day—whether it's a meal, a cup of coffee, or cuddling—so that you can catch up on the day's events and so that you don't become "two ships passing through the night."

Go to parties together or not at all. Force yourself to go to his distant cousin's wedding even though you don't know anyone and have a million things to do that weekend. If he's not in the mood to go to your friend's New Year's Eve party, don't force him to and don't go alone. Be willing to rent a video and order in Chinese food if he wants to ring in the New Year quietly.

Take your husband's opinion into consideration before buying things or making decisions that affect both of you. For example, before plunking down your credit card for a Laura Ashley bedspread and matching curtains, ask him if he likes that kind of frilly stuff. Do not assume men have no interest in such things. You might be surprised to find out that married men have very definite opinions about everything from time spent apart to decorating.

We have many married girlfriends and can tell you that their husbands are downright offended when they are not consulted about everything from the hemline of the cocktail dress they just bought to health and career issues. Married men can get particularly peeved if they find out that you consulted your friend or mother for advice and not them. They have egos and would like to think that they have the answers, that they are your savior, or at least that you care about their opinions enough to ask.

Separate vacations have become more popular among married couples. We don't think this is a good idea. Over time, doing your own thing will cause you to lead separate lives. We are not talking about a three-day trip to Florida with your sister or best friend—if you want to take small trips like this, feel free to. But if you want to take a major vacation—say, to spend two weeks in Europe—your husband should be your travel companion. But suppose your idea of a fun vacation is going to Europe or lying on the beach in the Caribbean, while your husband loves tours of historic sites and museums. Our advice is to figure out a way to do a little of both. One year, you can go to the beach, the next year you can do a tourist package together, or go on a trip with a beach near some sites of cultural interest. Once you start planning separate vacations, you become like roommates, not lovers.

Ditto for money. With more women working these days, it's become popular for couples to have separate savings or checking accounts instead of (or in addition to) a joint account. The idea is for each spouse to have his own "personal" money to spend without having to explain or account to the other. We are not financial experts and we don't presume to tell you how to save or spend your money in a marriage. There are plenty of books on that subject you can read. But we can tell you that couples we've counseled who pool their money and spend it as if they are a team generally do not have the money issues that plague couples with separate accounts. The reason? When you have a separate account, you're thinking "me," like a single person with a roommate. When you have a joint account, you're thinking "we," you're thinking unselfishly of what's best for both of you and your children, you have a common vision, similar goals. Whenever we ask a woman why she feels it necessary to put aside x amount of money from her paycheck in a separate account every month, she will invariably say, "That way I can buy a new dress or shoes without a hassle and without feeling guilty. . . . My husband thinks it's frivolous, that we should be spending every penny we have on the mortgage or our children's college tuition."

Our question is: What kind of marriage do they have if she is not allowed to spend a reasonable amount of money on herself, especially if she is earning it? When you have separate accounts it creates a whole secrecy about spending. Why can't she simply tell her husband, "I need a new dress," and take it out of their joint account? Similarly, a husband might set up a separate account to indulge his boat habit. Why does he need a separate account? If their marriage is a good one and he is not being irresponsible—not leaving bills unpaid in order to pay for the boat—why can't his wife be happy that he likes boating and be okay with the expenses that go along with it?

Another common response is, "What if our marriage doesn't work out? I want to make sure I have some money of my own." We have a problem with that, too. If a woman is going into a marriage with thoughts of "what if it doesn't work out," how committed can she be? Her problem is not money, but commitment or love.

If your primary objective is maximum financial independence and security, then yes, you should keep money on the side and have separate accounts. But if this is your primary objective, you should be reading a different book. This book is not about money, but what makes for a great marriage, and as far as we are concerned that includes complete trust about everything, even money. You should be able to place implicit trust in the fact that you are a team, that what's good for one is good for the other, and that the marriage is characterized by a generosity of spirit, not a nickel-and-dime mentality. It does not matter if you are poor or rich, it's about whether or not you trust your husband. Of course, we are not talking about gamblers, drug addicts, dishonest businessmen or men who are completely irresponsible—if you are married to one of these men, you will need to proceed with caution in many more areas of your marriage than money. No, we are talking about the average husband whom you married for richer or poorer. If you are worried about how your husband is spending or investing your money, then your problem is trust. If you don't trust your husband, you shouldn't have married him.

In our first book, we said not to go dutch treat, not because you can't afford to pay for dinner, but because any man who asks you to pay is probably not in love with you. If he's thinking about the cost of the shrimp dish you ordered then he's not thinking about you. The same applies to money matters in a marriage. If you're even thinking about money in a he-versus-me way and keeping score of who is earning what and spending what, there is something deeply wrong. The fact is, sometimes a wife has to support her husband through graduate school or a layoff or career change; sometimes a husband has to be the sole breadwinner when his wife decides to quit work to be a stay-at-home mom. Sometimes you earn more, sometimes he does. So what? Aren't you in this together? If you think in terms of all for one and one for all, there is no resentment or competition or need for separate accounts.

There are, of course, extenuating circumstances for keeping your money separately—for example, if you are divorced and have money from your first marriage that you are saving for your children, or have signed a prenuptial agreement. We have no problem with prenups. If either of you made tons of money before you met, why shouldn't you keep it? And if you have decided before your marriage that this is what you would do with your previous earnings, then it was a mutual decision, which is really the most important thing when it comes to money!

Rule #7: ─────────────────────

Give Him Fifteen Minutes Alone When He Comes Home

If you didn't figure this out when you were dating, then you'll find out pretty quickly when you're married. Men tend to like to be left alone, unless they indicate otherwise. So when your husband comes home from work, don't rush to the door and bombard him with questions, problems, and/or chores. He will feel smothered, like he's living with an overbearing mother, and might even start taking the long way home. Of course, you can give him a quick kiss hello—but then leave him alone.

For all you know, he had a bad day at work, got stuck in traffic, and spilled tomato sauce on his favorite tie during a client lunch and the last thing he wants to hear about is the leak in the bathroom and Junior's homework. So give him a break unless there's an urgent reason—such as your child is sick. Let him take off his jacket, sort through the mail, grab a cold drink, play with the dog, sit in his La-Z-Boy, or lie down on the couch for fifteen minutes before you say a word. If he's late coming home, don't stand by the door waiting to explode. Don't make him feel like he has to punch a clock at home. Find something to do while he unwinds.

It's always a better conversation when he looks around the house to see what you're up to and speaks to you first. He won't be moody and you'll feel better that you waited. If you also work and want to chill out before spending time with your husband and children, you can stop off at the gym for a quick workout on the way home, meditate on the bus or train, or listen to soothing music in your car. That way, you can relax on your own, and still give him his time to relax when he comes home.

Rule #8:

Be Supportive

How do you and your husband send each other off to work every day? Do you yell, "Have a good day!," from the other side of the house as he's walking out the door? Do you admonish, "Call me if you're going to be late for dinner?" Do you rush him out the door with, "Go already or you'll miss the train?" Do you even bother to say goodbye or kiss him? When your husband announces a career change, a financial investment, or starts a new diet, do you take a skeptical "wait and see" attitude?

If the above describes you more or less, you are doing your husband—and your marriage—a disservice. You should treat your husband like a warrior who is going out to battle every day. Rally him on. It's a jungle out there and he needs your support. Be his cheerleader. The next time he goes to work, give him a big smooch, a pat on the back, and a few words of encouragement. Any of the following will do:

"Good luck with your sales call."

"Knock 'em dead with your presentation."

"Kill the competition."

"I know you'll get that account and if you don't they're idiots!"

"You can do it!"

"I'm rooting for you."

"I want to hear all about the case when you come home."

If every man were sent to work with a big vote of confidence, productivity would skyrocket. Every man needs someone to build his ego—he can't count on his boss, his clients, his friends, or kids to do it. You're it! It's up to you! Pump him up the most when he is not doing so well. It's easy to believe in a man when he's just been promoted or is making a ton of money, but what about when he's just scraping by?

Let's say your husband is an aspiring comedy writer who makes his living driving a cab. When you were dating you laughed at all his jokes and told him that you knew he was going to be the next Jay Leno. It's been five years since your last vacation, and your support is waning. You're on the verge of saying, "Forget comedy and get a regular job like your cousin the CPA."

We know how you feel, but saying it will do more harm than good. And it won't work. Unless your husband has expressed an interest in accounting or quitting comedy, do not play career counselor. Keep laughing at his jokes and being supportive—unless of course you are starving and can't pay the rent. Remember your wedding vows. Do not be a fair-weather wife. Let's say your husband just announced that he is leaving his comfortable corporate job to start his own software business. There go the paid vacations and health insurance. He's working longer hours for less money, spending your joint savings on computers, fax machines, and phones, but he's convinced he's going to be the next Bill Gates. You're not exactly a happy camper. You want to scream, "So what was so bad about your corporate job?" Bite your tongue or he will think that you do not believe in him. Your entrepreneurial husband needs your encouragement. How would you like it if he disapproved of your "silly" decision to leave a high-paying job to work at home just because you didn't show a profit right away?

Even if your husband is full of himself, he should be allowed to dream. Let him. Don't burst his bubble. Why would any man want to come home to a wife who rolled her eyes and said, "Right!," every time he had an idea or made a resolution?

Maybe your husband wants to run for local political office. You know he doesn't have a prayer. He's running anyway. You want to say, "You've got to be kidding!" But in this case he doesn't want to hear the truth. He wants your support. So give it to him. Call all your friends and tell them to vote for him, stand by his side when he gives speeches, buy buttons and balloons and throw him a campaign party. It doesn't matter if he wins or loses, what matters is that you believe in him.

We know what you're thinking. This is all very childish. But men can be childish, sometimes, so just go along with it if you want to make your marriage strong. Don't be a party pooper.

Maybe your husband is going on his fifth diet this year.

You want to say, "And what's going to make this one any different?" His diets usually last about three weeks and end in donut binges at two o'clock in the morning. On his last diet, he actually *gained* three pounds. You have every right to be cynical. The facts speak for themselves. But your husband will appreciate some amnesia on your part and undying support, even if you have to act a little. Say, "Great! How can I help you? Do you want me to throw out the bread? Stock up on tuna? Make you lunch every day? I know you can do it." This isn't being dishonest, it's being kind. If bursting a man's bubble would make him earn more money or lose weight, then we'd say do it. But it doesn't. It crushes his ego and creates resentment. Being supportive is no guarantee your husband will be a success, but it will boost his confidence and improve your relationship.

Support him in everything. If your husband has a cold or sore throat, don't minimize it. Pay attention to him. Baby him. Make him his favorite soup, offer to get him medicine. If his favorite football team loses, show empathy, even if you couldn't care less. He will appreciate it. Don't forget to thank him and praise him whenever possible, when he takes out the garbage, mows the lawn, or hangs a picture on the wall. Make him feel needed and good about himself. Remember, behind every great man is a supportive wife! If you appreciate him, he'll do even more! And if you believe in him, he's more likely to believe in himself—and in you. He'll want to make you proud. And you will be.

Let Him Win

You fell in love with a house you really can't afford; he would rather buy a smaller house and have more money for furniture and a new car. You want to go first-class to Paris for your tenth wedding anniversary, he said okay, but never mentioned it again and your eleventh anniversary is just around the corner. You want to have three kids, he's fine with two. You want a luxury car; he wants to buy a compact and save money for the kids' college tuition.

Do you fight for what you want or let him win? Women ask us this all the time.

We say, unless it is a crucial issue to you, let him win. The relationship as a whole is more important than always getting your way. Better to be happy than always be right.

You may think we are being unfair. We know how you feel, but we are telling you what works. If you win and the relationship suffers, you lose, so is it really worth it?

We don't think so. Our experience is that even if you get your way, you will usually regret it. If you let him win, he can never say, "I told you so," or resent your forcing the issue.

You can probably relate to this true story: Marianne and Chuck fell in love with a house about $50,000 above their price range. Marianne wanted it no matter what. Chuck was reluctant, knowing that buying it would mean breaking into their IRAs and children's college savings. They continued to look at other houses, but Marianne talked day and night about the "dream" house. She told Chuck she wouldn't mind cutting back on expenses, going out to eat less, driving their old cars, and buying used furniture if they could live in that house. "If we don't eat out or go on vacation, we'll save thousands," she told him. After several weeks of persuasion, Chuck relented and bought the house, thinking it would make his wife happy.

It did for a while, but once they settled in, Marianne had a hard time adjusting to their new poverty status. There was no money to decorate the house, no money for a gardener. Chuck had to mow the lawn on his only day off. The kitchen appliances were old and needed to be replaced, but there was no money for new ones. Suddenly the reality hit her. In retrospect, Marianne wished she had waited for a house they could really afford.

Chuck never said "I told you so," but he grumbled about the heating bill and mowing the lawn, and Marianne felt guilty. They had also cut back on nice Saturday night dinners out, which in the past had given them some alone time to bond. Thus, the house took its toll on their marriage not only financially, but emotionally. The lesson here: It's never a good idea to force your will.

Karen always wanted to go to Italy. Her husband, Tim, had no interest in Europe; his idea of a fun vacation was Atlantic City or Las Vegas—poker, a concert, and buffet dinners. When Karen brought up Italy, he didn't want to disappoint her by saying no, so he pretended to go along with the idea, but had no plans to actually call a travel agent and didn't. He was hoping she'd forget or change her mind. She didn't pick up the hint. When a man drops a subject, you should take notice.

Karen didn't. Every week or two she asked Tim when he wanted to take the vacation and if he had called the travel agent. Tim kept coming up with excuses—work was busy, he didn't know if he could get away, he'd call tomorrow, next week. Karen finally confronted him, "So you don't really want to go to Italy, do you?" Tim said, "Well, if you really want to . . ." It was Karen's lifelong dream to see Rome and eat in sidewalk cafés. She was going to go whether Tim liked it or not.

So she made the arrangements and they went! Although Karen started out enjoying the trip, each time she looked over at Tim's glum expression, she felt worse, to the point where she could barely enjoy her pasta or the beautiful museums. Tim was tense and so was she. Looking back, she wished she had let it go. She could have come up with a compromise vacation where they would have both relaxed and enjoyed it.

If you are constantly at odds with your husband to have your own way on a particular issue, maybe it's time to step back and think why you must have it and what it is doing to your relationship. More often than not, when you let your husband be right and try to make him happy, he turns around and reacts in kind—and both of you win.

Of course, some issues are more crucial than expensive homes and lavish vacations. If the subject is truly important to you, we believe you should fight for what you want as long as you can live with the consequences—an angry husband, tension at home, or all-out warfare. You can't fight about *everything* though, so be choosy.

April had a situation which was too important for compromise: she had two boys and desperately wanted a girl. She tried to convince her husband Phil to try to have a third child. She bought books about conceiving a girl and talked incessantly about it. Phil had always wanted two. He didn't care about the sex of the child, but he didn't feel emotionally or financially comfortable having a third. We empathize with women in April's situation. Do you make yourself happy or do you make him comfortable?

April convinced Phil to go for it. They had a girl, but she could not get him to be involved in raising the child. He was a devoted parent to his two boys, but he rarely had the time or energy for the newborn. She changed just about every diaper and was the only parent up at night when the baby cried. No surprises here. April got what she wanted, but she was also saddled with all the work. Sometimes when you win, you still don't get everything you want or it takes a toll on your marriage. Remember to pick your battles carefully!

Rule #10: _____

Accept that Some Things Are None of Your Business

Every man has a few secrets or things he does that he does not want to be questioned about. As long as they are relatively harmless (not a drug addiction, alcoholism, compulsive gambling, infidelity, or tax evasion), don't demand that he tell you. You can gently feel him out to see if he is comfortable discussing any of the topics below, but if he wants his privacy, grant him that. (After all, you probably have a few secrets too.) Here are areas where it would be wise to mind your own business:

His relationship with (or lack of relationship with) his family. Don't ask him why he tells his mother everything or why he never talks to her. Focus on your own family— your relationship with *your* parents and children.

How long it really takes him to get home from work. You know it should take twenty minutes, but somehow he doesn't get home for a full hour. Don't ask him why. He may have met a friend for a quick drink or stopped off at Staples to buy pens, gone tie-shopping at Macy's or had the car washed. He doesn't want to have to account for every minute of his commute. You're not his mother! Remember, the time between work and home is about the only time he has to himself all day. It's the only time no one—not his boss, his clients, his kids, you—is bothering him, so let him enjoy it. When he comes home a little late, don't press him—just act glad to see him and enjoy your time together.

Business secrets. Some men would rather not tell you exactly what they have to do to make a sale or succeed in business. We're not talking about anything dishonest or illegal here. We're just saying they don't want to divulge the gory details of having to wine and dine a client to get their business or what pressure tactics they have to use. Your stockbroker husband doesn't want to tell you how he goes through the phone book to get people to invest their savings. Sometimes he'd rather not relive the transactions—it's enough to go through them at work! If your husband doesn't volunteer details about his business methods, assume you're not supposed to know.

His health. Some men don't go to a doctor or a dentist for years. They have a macho attitude or think, "if it ain't broke, don't fix it." Maybe they don't go because they don't want to hear the doctor say, "stop smoking, lose weight, exercise," or anything else they don't want to do. Some wait for a heart attack or an ulcer to go for a checkup. If you are married to a man who doesn't take care of his health, you can nicely ask him if he's due for a checkup, but do not nag him to go or make an appointment for him—you're not his mother! His health is his business, even if he is your husband. If your husband is overweight, don't ask him how much he weighs or sneak up behind him when he stands on the bathroom scale. If he doesn't volunteer the number, it's none of your business. You can, however, set a good example by eating healthy and exercising yourself. But that's about all.

How much he sleeps and his TV habits: Some men sleep too much (all weekend) or too little (four hours a night). It's not your job to correct either. Don't try to be the sleep cop. Some men fall asleep watching late-night TV, which can drive their wives crazy. But you can't reason with a man who insists on watching the *Tonight Show* every night but falls asleep in his La-Z-Boy chair before the monologue is even finished. As long as he spends time with you before this, don't question it.

How he dresses. Some women are embarrassed by their husband's wardrobe. Some men just don't know how to dress; some don't care about fashion or refuse to spend the money on good clothes; some wear clothes that are out of style because they hate shopping; and some wear clothes that don't fit well because they are out of shape. All you can do is help your husband dress if he asks you to and buy him ties, shirts, and suits as presents and put them in his closet. After that, you have to let it go. He's not ten years old. You can't make him look good or always wear what you want. Hopefully, he will like what you pick out for him as gifts—if not, just shrug it off as "his unique style."

Rule #11: _____

Try Not to Call Him too Much at Work

When you were dating your husband, you probably didn't call him that much, especially if you were following *The Rules.* Now that you're married, you probably call him whenever you feel like it. And this may be too much.

As we said in *The Rules,* it's always a better phone call if he calls you. Why? He's not in the middle of a meeting or deadline, he's in the mood to talk, he doesn't sound harried or gruff. When you call your husband at work and he sounds busy or gets off the phone quickly, you may feel hurt. So unless you really have to talk to him for a specific reason, wait until he calls you or talk to him when he comes home.

"Just because you have the ring doesn't mean you get to call your husband fifty times a day at work and whine about when he is coming home or that you miss him. Unless your child is sick or you won the lottery, leave him alone. Besides, you should be too busy to chitchat on the phone all day," says one happily married *Rules* wife.

Here are more suggestions:

Don't call just because you're feeling bored.

Don't call to complain about your job or him or anything for that matter.

Don't call to discuss your child's third-grade homework—that can wait until he comes home.

Don't call to get his attention.

Here's one great reason to call: to flirt about sex. This call should run about two minutes. Let him know he'll have a great night tonight! He'll have a terrific day just thinking about it—and you can bet he'll try to hurry home that night!

Rule #12: _____

Rarely Return His Gifts

Don't return your fiancé's or husband's gifts unless you absolutely can't look at them and are positive that you will never wear them! If the gift is passable—just not exactly the shape, design, or color you would have picked out yourself—tell him you love it and keep it for the sake of his feelings. Better to forgo your personal taste than hurt him.

Women like to think that men are made of steel with no feelings or sentimentality, and that a man really doesn't care if you keep his gift or exchange it. This couldn't be further from the truth. In fact, men get hurt and feel emasculated when you reject what they feel are their tokens of love, whether or not they admit it.

We are not being old-fashioned or sticklers for etiquette here. We know that times have changed. Years ago, most women wouldn't think of returning or exchanging a gift and gladly wore even repulsive-looking heirlooms. Today, women are more likely to discuss and even pick out their jewelry with their girlfriends or mothers or sisters before their own husbands. It is quite common to go ring shopping as a couple; surprises are a thing of the past. But if you want to make your husband happy, try to keep what he gives you. Our friend Marsha found this out the hard way.

Marsha had her heart set on a pear-shaped diamond engagement ring, so when her fiancé proposed with a round one, she said yes to the proposal and no to the ring. At first, Dave was shell-shocked and thought she was being heartless, but he eventually agreed that it was her ring and she should get what she wanted. Marsha got the pear, but her husband never forgot that she turned in the ring he spent weeks shopping for. Every time he thought of buying her jewelry for her birthday, Valentine's Day, or their anniversary, he wondered if she was going to return it. She did. For their first anniversary, he bought her a locket, but she didn't like the chain and exchanged it. He started to joke that she should just buy herself gifts and give him the bills. But beneath the humor was hurt and he no longer enjoyed buying her gifts. He feels a little bitterness on these occasions.

Years later, Marsha regrets changing the ring. Every time she looks at the pear, she knows it wasn't the ring Dave picked out and she feels bad about it. But the damage is done. She got what she wanted, but at a price. That's why we say try to put your husband's feelings before your personal taste.

Jane's motives were better, but the damage was the same. While Marsha was simply picky, Jane wanted to save money. When her husband bought her a $2,000 diamond necklace for their second anniversary, she said, "Bill, this is beautiful, but don't you think we should use the money for a new washing machine and dryer? Ours are on their last leg."

Jane thought Bill would be thrilled—after all, how many wives would forgo diamonds for appliances? On the contrary, Bill was upset and insisted she keep the necklace, which she did begrudgingly. Their anniversary was somewhat tainted by Jane's lack of graciousness. She thought she was being helpful and that his priorities were misplaced. But that's because she didn't understand her husband's mentality. Without meaning to hurt Bill's ego, she managed to criticize his role as breadwinner, implying that he couldn't take care of the house and shower her with diamonds at the same time.

Like Jane, some married women deny themselves in the name of fiscal prudence. They're always trying to cut costs, so when their husbands say, "What would you like for your birthday?," they say "Nothing" or "Don't bother." Men don't appreciate that. They want to give you something. It feeds their ego. When you wear their jewelry, you're saying "I'm yours." So if you are anything like Marsha or Jane, when your husband gives you a gift, keep it. When he asks what you want, smile and say, "Whatever you get will be great," or give him a tiny hint. Remember, you are trying to make your husband happy, not pass a lie-detector test.

Don't Expect a Lot of Sympathy from Your Husband

Have you ever felt sick and sought solace from your husband? Were you disappointed that he wasn't more sympathetic? Did you regret that you complained to him?

You're not alone. We've all been there and want to help you avoid being disappointed again. As absurd as this sounds, try not to take his lack of compassion personally. Your husband is not deliberately *trying* to be mean or uncaring. He doesn't even think he's being mean, he thinks he's being rational and that you're overreacting. In fact, he thinks he's being *helpful* by calming you down and being the voice of reason.

The fact is, he's just a man and for thousands of years men have been raised to keep a stiff upper lip, not to cry or complain too much. Where do you think the phrase "take it like a man" came from? Consequently, men don't call their best friend when they have the flu. They just stay home, wear an old bathrobe, watch TV, and suffer in silence. (It is very common for husbands to let down their guard with their wives, but that's because they trust you won't tell anyone. Don't make a joke out of it to them— or anyone else—as he'll feel betrayed, especially since he probably has *no* idea he has been complaining and feeling sorry for himself.)

By contrast, most women will tell everyone they know and even strangers in the supermarket line that they have their period. Women bond over sickness—"The cramps are unbelievable." Men bond over success—"I just won another account"—or sports—"The Yankees won!" We are not making this up. We have heard many stories from countless wives over their husbands' seeming heartlessness.

For example, our friend Ronnie recalled eating something that upset her stomach right before going for a dental cleaning. She felt so sick that she threw up on the dental assistant. She called her husband on the way home to tell him what happened. His first words were, "That must have been awful for her," meaning the assistant! He sounded more concerned about the assistant—then asked how his wife was feeling.

Another friend, Patricia, called us one evening to say that when she told her husband that she had a migraine headache during dinner, his answer was, "Will it away, will it away!"

A woman we know by the name of Margie suffers from severe menstrual cramps. Three days before her period is due she can barely move and when the bleeding starts she has to lie down a lot for about four days. Her husband finds it hard to believe that her period can be so bad. Even though he has obviously never had this problem to know for sure, is not a gynecologist, has two brothers (no sister), and never lived with a woman to know what *her* period was like, he is sure that his wife's pain can't be that bad and tells her so every month. "I've spoken to experts and they say your period shouldn't be that debilitating," he recently told her.

Marcia is a freelance magazine writer and stay-at-home mom. She recalled having a deadline on a major story the same day her baby-sitter canceled. She spent the day interviewing sources and typing furiously while keeping her four-year-old at bay with snacks and Play-Doh. She feared that one wrong move and his apple juice would spill on her computer and cause it to crash. When her husband came home and asked, "How was your day?," she said, "Really hard, the baby-sitter canceled and I had a tight deadline." "Okay, but you got through it, right?" he said matter-of-factly.

Another harried businesswoman claimed that when she complained to her husband about her long hours and job frustrations, he told her, "You've got to take the Eisenhower approach—radiate optimism at all costs." She wanted to hear, "God, they're really overworking you." She did not bother to tell him that he made her feel even worse.

You might think that we are talking only about mathematical types—aerospace engineers, Wall Street analysts, or software programmer husbands, but we are not. We know women who are married to doctors, men in the healing profession, even psychiatrists who are just as unsympathetic. We are not trying to be men-bashers here.

We are just pointing out one fairly typical weakness—a poor bedside manner. Is it any wonder that more men aren't nurses?

Most men can be very understanding about other things. For example, tell the average man that you don't know how to balance your checkbook and he will sit down with you and a calculator for hours until your finances are in order. But tell a man that you feel sick or that the women in the neighborhood are catty and he'll think you should just have a better attitude. Have you ever heard a man complain that he's too sick to play basketball or that the men in his office aren't friendlier?

We are not advising you not to confide in your husband, just don't be surprised or get angry at him if you don't get the attention and nurturing you were looking for. Thank goodness for friends and relatives!

Rule #14: —————————————————

Rules for Fighting

Did you ever have a fight that began because he didn't change the toilet paper and suddenly you found yourself saying things like, "I'm sorry I married you. I do everything around here, the place would fall apart without me!"

Before you know it, you're ranting about everything you can think of, every disappointment or every one of his screwups—like the time he was a month late buying you a birthday present, the hotel room he forgot to reserve on your last vacation, how you always have to remind him to take out the garbage and pay the Visa bill. When you run out of material about him, you find fault with his best friend or his good-looking secretary. "It's interesting how all the secretaries in your company are ex-models!"

Even the most loving couples have been known to fight like this, even though it's terribly damaging and gets them nowhere. Sometimes it takes days or weeks to recover from these fights, but invariably they're at it again.

But it doesn't have to be that way. Since you're the one reading this book, not your husband, it's up to you to take the high road.

Here are ten rules to keep the warfare to a healthy minimum:

1. Keep your fight to the subject at hand. In this case, "I would appreciate it if you could remember to replace the toilet paper." End of subject.
2. Call it quits if either of you start to stray from the subject at hand.
3. Don't attack his character. Don't say, "You're such a slob, I'm always picking up after you." Just address the problem, not the person.
4. Agree to disagree. What's a big deal to you—a perfect bathroom—isn't to him.
5. Don't make threats—"Maybe I should stay with my mother for a week and we'll see if the toilet paper ever gets changed or if anything else gets done around here." Before you know it, you're threatening to leave him for a week over toilet paper!
6. Don't let yourself be provoked. If he says, "Why should I have to, what do you do all day anyway? How hard is it to change the toilet paper?," don't respond, just leave the room. If you react angrily, he will think "there she goes again, getting mad over nothing." If you say nothing, he will probably apologize later for being mean or unfair. Don't be vengeful. Don't sleep in another room (or ask him to) that night because you're in a fight. (You should only sleep in another room if he snores too loud or one of

you has to wake up in the middle of the night for a business trip.)

7. Switch gears. Go for a walk or call a friend.
8. Think "What would I be doing if I weren't fighting with him?" Go do it.
9. Think loving thoughts.
10. Think "How important is it?" and move on.

Better yet, the next time your husband doesn't change the toilet paper, change it yourself and don't say a word. Remember there are plenty of things your husband does—taking out the garbage, refinancing the mortgage, paying the bills, having the car fixed—that he doesn't expect you to do or even tell you about.

So let it go. Life is not fair. Don't be a bean-counter, keeping score of everything you do versus what he does. Everything evens out in the end. Haven't you ever had a friend where one year it's all about her problems and the next year it's all about yours? Marriage is just like that— it all works out in the end.

Say What You Mean, But Don't Say It Meanly

You don't always have to hit your husband over the head with a hammer to be heard. Sometimes you can get what you want by just asking or making your case *nicely!* Here are some suggestions:

You want to say, "When's the last time you gave me a backrub?" Instead say, "I'd love a backrub." This is called speaking from the "I" and it works. You ask for what you need without calling him selfish. You get what you give.

Or you want to say, "You look terrible in that orange shirt." Instead say, "I think your blue shirt really brings out your eyes." It's always good to look at the bright side of things. He will appreciate the compliment. Who likes to be told they don't look good in something?

Your husband forgets to buy bread on his way home from work even though you reminded him three times that day. Don't say, "What a moron. How could you forget the bread? I guess I have to do everything around here myself." Say, "Next time, could you maybe write down 'bread' on a Post-it or e-mail yourself so you don't forget?"

You don't like his haircut. Don't say, "Your ears are sticking out. You look ridiculous." Say, "I know a great haircutter."

Your husband asks you to drive him to the airport for a business trip. Don't say, "I'm not your chauffeur." Say, "I really would if I could, but I have appointments all morning. How about if I call a cab?"

Your husband thinks that the filet mignon is not tender enough. Don't say, "If you don't like it, you can eat at a restaurant." Say, "Really? I like it this way, but I'll try not to cook yours as long next time."

You get the idea! There's a nice way and a mean way of saying just about anything! So why do we choose the mean way more often than not? Because we're frustrated, hurt, self-righteous, want to make a point, want revenge, or are in just a complete state of shock or disbelief at our husband's behavior and must let him know it. We want to beat him over the head with a sledgehammer, not a feather, so he hears us. Or we go to the other extreme and give him the silent treatment. You know, silent scorn. Both ways are extremely harmful to a relationship and can ruin an evening or a week or a month of your marriage. Remember the last time you were sarcastic or mean or critical, did it get you anywhere? Probably not.

The next time you're upset and want to say something mean, reread this chapter, take a deep breath, calm down, and think of a nice way of saying the same thing. You can actually turn this into a game you can play with your friends. Tell them what you want to say and ask them to help you figure out what you're going to say instead!

You may be thinking, "But this is so silly. What difference will a few words make?" Or you may think, "This is not being true to my feelings." We know exactly how you feel, we have felt that way too. But we learned to look at it this way: we have a higher self and a lower self. Telling the truth without consideration for another person's feelings is your lower self. There's an expression, truth without kindness is cruelty! Nobody, especially your husband, wants the so-called *truth* if the truth is you hate his clothes or wish he made more money.

So the next time you are about to say something hurtful, pause and think of how you can soften the blow. We guarantee you will feel better about yourself, your husband will appreciate your kindness, and you may just get what you want after all.

Rule #16: _____

Don't Use the D (Divorce) Word

How many times have you had a fight about something trivial and before you knew it, you were threatening divorce? You felt so angry, so hurt, so frustrated, so unloved in that moment that you didn't care what you said—the sky's the limit and you said the "D" word even though you didn't really mean it.

Why did you say it? Because you wanted your husband's attention. The D word has shock value. You want him to hear it and make up quickly or reassure you of his eternal devotion. You want him to say "Divorce? Don't be silly. I love you forever. Never say that word again."

The problem is, if you say it once for dramatic effect or reassurance, you'll say it every time you fight or want attention and before you know it, you'll be planting poison in your marriage. It will be in the air. And maybe one day you will act on your idle threats or he will. You reap what you sow. So if you don't *really* want a divorce, don't even say it. Take the word out of your vocabulary. Think about what you're saying when you've calmed down. Better to confide in a friend than to constantly chant, "divorce, divorce," until it has no meaning. If you carelessly throw the word around, you will have no credibility anyway.

Remember how we told you never to bring up the M (marriage) word when you were dating him? Well, ditto for the divorce word when you're married! Tell yourself "not allowed," it's hitting below the belt. Saying "divorce" in the middle of an argument is like a child saying "I don't want to play anymore." Rather than solving the problem in your marriage—whatever that may be on any given day—you are sending the message that you just want out, you don't want to play anymore, and that's childish. We are not judging anyone. Who has not behaved childishly at one time or another with spouses and loved ones? Is there anyone who hasn't said mean, spiteful things, slammed doors, or walked out when the anger and hurt felt warranted? As everyone knows, love and hate are very close so it's only natural to feel hatred sometimes when someone you love has hurt you. The problem is, saying the mean, rotten things feels good for about a minute, but an hour or so later, you feel remorse. You can't just undo mean words you have spoken.

Saying "divorce" eventually backfires. Men tend to mirror what their wives say. So if you say, "we have a good marriage," your husband will think so too. If you constantly say how unhappy you are with him, he will think you are and think he is. So be careful what you say around your husband. We know women who constantly say how tired or unhappy they are, and how it's because of him—

and their husbands start to believe them. You are what you say, so choose your words carefully.

It's not only the divorce word that you must refrain from saying, but anything like it, such as, "I should never have married you anyway!" or "I'd be so happy if I never saw you again." Bad language should also be off-limits; it's just not ladylike or nice.

All of the above are not only hurtful, they can irreparably damage a marriage. There are some husbands who may forgive these outbursts, but they may never forget. Men tend to store bad stuff. They're not like women who can let it roll off their backs over lunch with a girlfriend or during a fun shopping spree.

So why take a chance and say the D word, especially if you probably don't mean it anyway? If you are prone to saying "divorce" and statements like that in your marriage, you must find an appropriate way to vent your anger—friends, therapist, support group—so that you don't do damage. In the next chapter, we suggest rules for fighting so that you don't have to resort to saying things you don't mean.

If you just said the D word yesterday or five minutes ago, apologize, but the best way to make amends is to not say it the next time you are tempted to. "Sorry" is never as effective as simply not saying it at all.

Don't Scream, Speak Softly

When it comes to men, it's not what you say, it's how loudly or softly you say it. And most men prefer that you say it softly. Say it softly and you have their complete attention. Scream and they tune out, pull the phone away from their ear, or leave the room, even if what you are screaming is right, true, and important. We asked a few men if screaming is ever a good idea and one said, "Yes, during sex!" That says it all.

Screaming at any other time reminds them of their mothers. "Clean your room!" "Eat your vegetables!" "Don't drive too fast." They just can't take that screeching sound.

Another reason not to scream is that it will make your husband focus on your anger instead of his bad behavior. For example, if he is on the computer all the time and you scream at him to help you around the house, he will say, "Why do you have to yell?," instead of "You're right, I haven't cut the shrubs like I promised you I would."

Screaming can also lead to violence—hitting and throwing things and breaking things and tearing important papers and photos, taking off your wedding ring, driving recklessly, who knows? Remember when you were dating your husband? Did you scream? Probably not. You were trying to impress him and get him to marry you, so you were on your best behavior. Try to be like that now even though he's yours. When you feel rage, take a deep breath, go for a walk if possible, or call a friend and talk through your anger until you can speak to your husband in a reasonable voice. (Cell phones are a real godsend. You can vent to your friends while going for a walk when you feel you're going to lose it with your husband!)

Don't think we are being superficial. Try speaking softly for a week or a month and see if your husband isn't more attracted to you. You might find this hard to do at first. It is exactly the opposite of what we think. We think if we speak louder, we will be heard. But the opposite is true. Speak softly and your husband will actually hear you.

This strategy is so simple that you may think it beneath you—especially if you are an aggressive lawyer or doctor or businesswoman—but it really works. We know one woman who practically purrs when she talks to her husband, which makes him respond as if he is madly in love with her, which he is. When she occasionally forgets her composure and raises her voice, he looks at her differently, like he married a witch. We are not making this up. This is what she told us.

Be especially careful around PMS time—before your

period when you are particularly irritable, hostile, and could easily shoot your husband if he brought home the wrong flavor of Haagen-Dazs. Circle the date you are expecting your period so you can anticipate and control your rage. We know one woman who was so hostile during PMS that her husband divorced her after two years. He just couldn't take the rage, the mood swings, and occasional violence.

What to do with the anger behind the screaming? Some women eat or drink it away and that's why they never scream. They use food and alcohol as tranquilizers to put on a happy face. Of course, we don't recommend either. It's self-destructive. You suffer—get fat or drunk—and whatever you are mad about doesn't get addressed.

Other women go to individual or group therapy, which is a good idea. But what if you want to scream at your husband on Tuesday at nine P.M. and your therapy sessions are Wednesday at two P.M.? What if your therapist is on vacation or unavailable?

If you're rich, you can spend a month at an anger-management clinic where you learn to share your fury with a staff of professional psychiatrists in between making beds and eating cafeteria food among other rage-aholics. But what if you can't afford an anger clinic or even a weekly therapist? What if you have a full-time job, three kids, food to buy, a house to clean and can't drop any of that to work on your anger? Since most married women are in your position, you have to do the best you can wherever you are. When you feel the urge to scream at your husband because he came home three hours late or forgot the milk that you had made a special call to remind him of, or procrastinates on chores around the house, call a girlfriend and tell her exactly what you plan to say to him until you feel calmer and can say it softly to your husband. You may have to call her twice to calm down—but so what? Anything's better than screaming. If no one's around, write down your feelings on paper until you feel the anger dissipate. Go for a walk or jump on the treadmill. Releasing endorphins is a good way to channel your angry energy and calm down.

Of course, doing all of the above means forgoing the satisfaction of screaming at your husband, which you may actually enjoy sometimes. Who doesn't love to scream when they feel justifiably angry? But you'll pay a big price. Your husband may start avoiding you, watch TV all the time, find reasons to stay at the office late, or look for soft-spoken women at bars and nightclubs!

Even if your husband puts up with your temper, has screaming ever gotten you anywhere? Has screaming ever made him "see the light," hear you, and change? Probably not. So the best reason to speak to your husband softly is that he will listen, which is what you wanted in the first place. And you will feel good about yourself, as opposed to feeling like a raving lunatic. Try it!

Rule #18: _____

To Compare Is to Despair— Don't Compare Him with Other Husbands

We all have friends whose husbands either make more money, have tighter abs, are more compassionate, have nicer parents, spend more time with their kids, or _____ (fill in the blank!). How many times have you innocently pointed out one attribute or another to your husband?

"You know Mark just bought Jill a Mercedes S.U.V. and they're going to Hawaii in January," you nonchalantly mention to your husband, despite the fact that you are still driving your seven-year-old station wagon and he's planning a camping trip.

"Adam made partner last week," you announce to your husband, whose position is being eliminated in a corporate merger.

"Peter runs five miles a day," you brag to your spouse who's thirty-five pounds overweight and uses the stationary bike you bought him to hang his tight-fitting trousers on.

"John really listens when Lisa talks."

"Bob is home every night for dinner."

"Jeff's parents baby-sit for their kids every weekend."

Do you recognize yourself in these comments? It's natural to slip from time to time, especially when you're feeling out of sorts or jealous. But you must try to hold your tongue. Your husband will not appreciate the commentary. And he might even get vicious and point out that Peter, the avid runner, has been out of work for months and that's why he has so much time to exercise.

If your husband is typical, he will rarely say "You're right" and strive to be more like Mark, Adam, Peter, or John. He will either deny that he's not a good listener or breadwinner, point out the flaws in the husbands you are gushing about, or remind you that you didn't marry someone rich, athletic, or whatever. He might get really angry and shout, "Then why didn't you marry him?" Or he might get even by reminding you how Jane works full-time yet manages to take care of three kids and is active on the PTA, while you are a stay-at-home mom with one child. Any way you look at it, you lose. So why go there? You will do more damage than good. We're not saying that your motives can't be pure. You may be genuinely worried about your husband's health and want to inspire him to be healthy and fit. Or you may want to nudge your lackadaisical spouse into being more ambitious at work for your family's future financial security. But it's more likely that you are angry and seeking revenge by trying to put your husband down. In either case, your tactic is sure to backfire.

So if you don't want to emasculate your husband and

possibly create ill feelings, try to refrain from pointing out the one or two qualities other married men have that your husband doesn't. Granted, we don't always mean to be hurtful when we say such things, we're just venting frustration, but it *is* hurtful and your husband is going to feel that he's not making you happy. You should always try to make your husband *think* he is making you happy. Believe it or not, the more he *thinks* he is making you happy, the harder he will try.

We live in a society riddled with envy, where comparing cars, homes, husbands, and incomes is all too common, especially if you have close couple friends and are privy to their lifestyles and finances. But try not to dwell on what you have versus what they have because it will only erode your marriage and make you forget all the wonderful reasons you married your husband. If you really need to vent, we suggest you find a good close-mouthed friend you can complain to, rather than your husband.

Better yet, try to catch yourself when you are even *thinking* about what you're not getting from your husband. When a negative thought comes to mind, quickly change your focus to a few of your husband's positive attributes or acts of kindness. (Remember the time he stayed up all night with you when you had food poisoning on your honeymoon?) You're less likely to say something awful if you change your thoughts to positive ones.

Also, if you take the time to sit still and think about why you compare at all, you might realize that the real issue is one of acceptance. Can you accept the fact that you don't get everything in one husband, even in your Mr. Right? It would be wonderful if we could all pick and choose the best qualities of every husband we know and roll them into our husband, but it doesn't work that way. If you want to be happy or at least content, you have to come to terms with the fact that he has strengths and shortcomings. As we all know, happiness isn't having what you want, but wanting what you have.

Rule #19: —————————————

Don't Ask Your Single Friends for Marital Advice

Remember the old grade school retort: It takes one to know one? Well, it's absolutely true. So when you absolutely have to vent about your husband or need marital advice, call a married girlfriend instead of a single one. No matter how smart or well-meaning your single friend is, you will get more effective advice and understanding from your married friends.

The problem with single friends is that they tend to have one of two perspectives: they either romanticize marriage, or they disdain it. The single friends who romanticize marriage don't realize that fighting is a normal part of life, that it is possible to have the most hateful thoughts toward the person you love the most, your spouse. They want to believe that marriage is like a perfume commercial. When you tell them about your fights, they can make you feel that you have marital problems. They might sound shocked by your anger or recommend marriage counseling. You want to say, no, really, it's not a big deal, we kiss and make up all the time, I'm just venting. But they will never understand until they are married.

Often these friends are so eager to get married that they can't imagine having a problem with Mr. Right. They think you should be walking on air twenty-four hours a day. If you call this type of single friend to complain about your husband, she'll show no sympathy. "Oh, leave him alone. You should consider yourself lucky to be married. I haven't had a good date in years. All the good guys are taken. I'll trade places with you any day!" You can try to explain to your friend that yes, you're grateful to be married, but being married isn't always perfect or easy. You may try to explain that you can't walk around like a Barbie doll every day just because you're married, and that even though you love your husband, he is a control freak. But it's no use, she doesn't get it. (She also might resent it that you are bothering her with your petty issues when she doesn't even have a Saturday night date and her irritability may come out in her answer.)

If you called a married girlfriend and complained about the same thing, she'd laugh and say, "I know, I know, I told Dave a hundred times to stop being so bossy, to save it for the office." You feel understood, you get perspective.

The other type of single friend—typically, the type who disdains marriage—thinks *you* can say or do no wrong, and that you should fight for your rights. "He never helps you around the house? I don't think you should put up with that, I certainly wouldn't if I were married. You do everything—shop, cook, clean—he could at least dry the dishes or something. I would make a list of chores for him to do. If he doesn't do them, well then he can eat off the floor," she would say in a militant voice. As you listen to her droning on, you know why she's not married. Compromise, the key to a successful marriage, is not in her vocabulary. If she wants to see a comedy and you want to see a romantic movie, she'd go by herself rather than join you just for the company. She's a good friend—you just wouldn't want to be married to her.

Your married friend would remind you that *most* husbands don't appreciate how much their wives do or think they know better, so why should yours be any different? She would also point out that the workload usually evens out in the end, so don't be a bean counter. After the call, you realize she's right and you don't feel like a victim.

Let's face it, your married friends have the experience and understanding that even your nicest, wisest single friends don't. They know that marriage is about compromise and making things work—that it's gray, not black or white. Single women can be wonderful friends, but we suggest you leave them out of it when you and your husband are having the fight of the week.

Rule #20: _____

Have a Family Dinner at Least Once a Week

In this frenetic world of beepers, cell phones, pagers, e-mail, on-line trading, Chinese takeout, and bad airline food, just about every husband craves a quiet dinner at home once a week or more. It doesn't matter if you cook up his favorite meal or order in, the point is to pick a night where everyone comes to the table at an agreed-upon hour and no one watches TV, listens to the radio, or calls or answers the phone.

By day, your husband is raiding corporations or living out of a suitcase, maybe even reading contracts and other documents when he goes to the bathroom, and trying to figure out when he's going to see his son play soccer, visit his mother in the nursing home, plan the vacation he hasn't had in five years—you get the idea.

By night, he wants a tranquil Norman Rockwell kind of dinner without headaches or crises from friends, family, or business associates and clients. Having a family dinner will make him feel like he's not just an automaton, not just a worker, but a family man. If he had a good childhood filled with family dinners, it will remind him of that. If he didn't have a good childhood, he will feel that you're making up for it. He will feel calm, that all is well with the world. For two hours, he can forget that his company is being taken over or that the stock market is down.

For that night, let him be the King of the Castle, even if you live in a one-bedroom. Serve him his favorite drink; don't let him lift a finger. You don't have to wear a dress or an apron, but just for one night try to be a little like June Cleaver. If he says, "Where's the ketchup or can I get a glass of water?" don't yell, "It's in the refrigerator, get up and get it yourself." Instead, walk over and give it to him, even if the refrigerator *is* closer to him. Be easygoing. Don't ask him to clear away his plate or help with the dishes. Let him feel like he's eating in a restaurant where everything is magically served and messes disappear. Whereas on other nights, you might get annoyed if he talks about business or local politics, on this night be happy to talk about whatever he wants. If you really aren't interested or have nothing to add to the conversation, just smile and listen. He will appreciate it. It's old-fashioned, some would say a little sexist, but it works! Try it!

This rule is not just good for your husband, but for you and your children. If you are a working mother, you are no doubt stressed out by the juggling act you have to perform every day. A weekly family dinner will give you a sense of belonging and togetherness. For one hour, you will not feel like a rat in a maze.

If you don't set aside one special night every week, you run the risk of being like strangers passing through the night, eating separately, not speaking for two days, and losing a sense of family. This can happen quite easily in our telephone-tag society. Don't let it happen to you.

Don't Force Him to Talk

It's no secret that women like to get their needs met and work through issues by talking things out while men are just as happy *not* talking. Most men are perfectly fine just hanging out and enjoying the quiet of their marriage, and assume everything is going well.

So if you like to talk and your husband doesn't, then we suggest you don't force the issue. Conversations are never as good when you coerce your husband to talk. In fact, a rather famous married couple once joked that the secret to their long, happy marriage was that they'd never had a deep conversation!

We are by no means suggesting that you hold back from having meaningful discussions or that you should suppress your vivacious personality, just that there are times when talking will do more harm than good. (Incidentally, by "not talking" we don't mean "the silent treatment" or "silent scorn," but a peaceful, pleasant silence—one that you both can enjoy.)

Definitely do not try to talk to him when he's on the computer, watching his favorite TV show or sporting event, or during sex, *especially during sex.* Sometimes women try to talk about the details of their day while they are being intimate with their husbands. A million little thoughts whirl through their heads and they want to blurt out, "Don't forget about the parent-teacher conference tomorrow" or "the lamp in the den exploded today."

Married life can become very busy and complicated and sometimes you just don't get a lot of time together and there are things you *really must* tell him, but figuring out when and how is crucial. Exercising self-restraint is everything.

Believe it or not, we know one married woman who picked up the phone while having sex because her girlfriend was having a crisis. Her husband certainly didn't appreciate that! Let her leave five messages on the answering machine and call her back a little later!

Don't be surprised if you have trouble following this rule. Most women equate physical bonding with verbal bonding, while men equate physical bonding with physical bonding. For them, less talk or even no talk means intimacy. So try to lose yourself in the moment. Or, if you can't, pretend you're an actress and your part is *not* to talk. A woman we know told us that just about every time she is quiet, her husband says, "I love you." Coincidence? We don't think so. Not talking will make you mysterious and interesting, which is always attractive to men. Try it and see what happens.

Another time not to talk is when you're fighting and

he doesn't want to continue the argument or you've hurt his feelings. Forcing a man to resolve issues on your timetable will only backfire. Your best bet is to leave him alone to sulk or think until he is ready to forgive and approaches you. Remember, silence can be golden.

Don't Hang on His Every Word

We know very attractive women who don't feel pretty when they are not dating anyone, or when the men they are dating stop calling. Conversely, we know less attractive women who feel pretty no matter what—single, married, or divorced.

If you are the kind of woman who feels good (or bad) depending on the last person you spoke to—whether it's a man, a friend, your mother, or your boss—don't think this kind of insecurity goes away when you're married. It doesn't, unless you really work at not hanging on your husband's every word.

For example, we know several married women who are easily hurt when their husbands criticize them. Mary Jo is one of them. Her husband, Tom, would frequently comment on her parenting skills. He was always looking over her shoulder when she was taking care of their two-year-old son. "Are you sure you're not giving him too much medicine? Is that sweater warm enough? It's really cold outside. Did you hear that cough? I think you should think twice about going out today." You get the idea. At times, Mary Jo was so hurt she couldn't even respond. At other times, she couldn't contain her anger and screamed, "Since you're so perfect, why don't you stay home and take care of him? Do you think I'm a moron? That I didn't measure the medicine I gave him?" When she erupted with anger, it made matters worse. Her husband would look at her in disbelief. "Why are you getting so upset? I didn't say you were doing anything wrong. I was just trying to help. God, you're so sensitive!" Of course, that only made her feel twice as bad. She thought, I'm not a good mother *and* I'm too sensitive!

No matter what Mary Jo did, she always felt inadequate. Even though she constantly consulted her pediatrician, married friends, and baby books for advice and all reassured her that she was doing everything right, she never felt good enough. Because her husband never gave her the praise she was looking for, she believed him, and thought everyone else must be too lenient or plain wrong.

Here is what we told Mary Jo and other women in similar situations. Don't hang on your husband's every word. If you know you're a good mother, your husband's comments are no reflection on you! Maybe this is his way of being involved. Maybe his father did the same thing to his mother. Whatever. Detach, don't take it personally. You can then either ignore the advice or take it if he has any good suggestions—maybe the sweater isn't warm enough.

Easier said than done, of course. But over time, Mary Jo came to see a pattern. It wasn't just her husband who made her feel she was not good enough. If her mother found fault with her housekeeping or her friend didn't like how she decorated the house, she felt they were right and she was wrong. We suggested she start saying affirmations like, "What other people think of me is none of my business." "Everybody has an opinion, so what?" "I'm enough, what I do is enough." At first she didn't believe any of it, but she kept saying these phrases until she felt stronger. The more she worked on developing an inner core of confidence, the less she cared what anyone said.

Perhaps your issue is not parenting, but something else. Maybe your husband thinks you spend too much money or that you're bad with finances. He's constantly on your case to balance your checkbook and grills you about every new purchase to make sure you're going to really use it. "Is that treadmill for hanging clothes?" he asks. Consequently, you feel that he must be right even though you always clip coupons, have never bounced a check, and are a relentless comparison shopper. As long as you know in your heart that you are not trying to waste money, you can go about your business guilt-free.

Here's a classic case of taking your husband's every word too much to heart: You come home with a new hairdo or outfit and ask your husband, "How do I look?" If he says, "Fine," you moan: "Just fine?" He says, "It's really nice." You want to hear "gorgeous," "sexy," "stunning," but he doesn't say those words and suddenly you don't feel pretty. You look in the mirror and the same outfit that you fell in love with at the store looks lousy. You can't decide whether you look good anymore. You feel low and confused, not to mention hurt and unattractive.

What to do? Well, if you don't want to go through this torture, don't ask your husband what he thinks. Just wear the outfit and if he notices fine, if he doesn't, fine. Don't look for attention. Stop caring so much what he thinks and you won't be so hurt. Maybe he's in a funk and doesn't feel like talking about your clothes. Just leave him alone.

Even if your husband is the type to lavish compliments on you, you can't live on that. If you feel good only when he tells you how sexy or smart you are, then how will you feel when one day he tells you to firm up your thighs or complains that all you do is talk on the phone with your friends? If you're happy because he says you're wonderful, then you'll be unhappy when he forgets to say it. Get in the habit of praising yourself and you will feel good about yourself, which is all that matters anyway.

Do Things You Don't Want to Do

Being married has a lot of benefits—no more lonely Saturday nights or vacations alone; a love in your life, a companion, someone to grow old with, to name a few—but it's not a free ride. You just can't have your old single life and him too. At times, you may have to do things you would never do if you weren't married to him. You may have to compromise about who you see, where you go, and what you do.

Most women rebel like a two-year-old when their husbands suggest going to a basketball game or renting a sci-fi film. "No way!" They push for massages at the health club or a romantic comedy. Or they go along begrudgingly and their husbands can't help but notice their scowl or frown. All of this is wrong, of course. But you can't blame yourself. Everything we read these days says "take care of yourself," "you come first," "do what's good for you." That's all well and good, but it's not great advice for marriage.

We recommend just the opposite. Go along with many of the things he wants and be easy to be with, as long as it doesn't harm you and you're not too sick to go. He will appreciate it so much and your marriage will be better for it. We have found that any sacrifices you make will come back to you tenfold in marital bliss. Don't feel sorry for yourself or think that you're the only one. Women who marry public figures, celebrities, politicians, and CEOs have to host or attend all kinds of fund-raisers, award shows, and dinner parties, and meet and greet strangers almost every day when they'd rather spend time alone or with their family or friends. When you are married, your life is no longer completely your own. You can grumble about it or put a smile on your face. It's up to you.

Here are ten suggestions:

1. If he likes to go to football games and/or college reunions that you have absolutely no interest in, pretend it's a job and go. Get all dressed up, plaster a smile on your face, meet and greet his friends, endure frigid temperatures and bad food at stadiums and auditoriums, wear the name tag, and make small talk with his friends' wives. Don't be a party pooper. Don't look at your watch a lot or ask him ten times "Are you ready to go now?"

2. Be willing to be the last to leave his nephew's bar mitzvah or uncle's wedding when he wants to catch up with *all* 250 guests. Be an actress. Show interest in his family. Talk to Uncle Lou about his fishing trip and ask Aunt Hannah about her hip surgery. Ask his grandmother to dance. Don't roll your eyes a lot and

look miserable. Ditto for business dinners with his boss and his boring wife.

3. Wear a miniskirt and high heels on Saturday night when you'd rather wear jeans and flats because you know it would make him happy. Be flattered that he wants to look at *your* legs, not somebody else's. Trust us, he's either looking at you or someone else, so let it be you! In the summer, wear a bikini if he likes that or whatever bathing suit he finds sexy. When you're out with him, try to dress for him, not for other women.

4. Watch an X-rated video with him if he wants you to, even if you find such stuff vulgar and boring. Be flattered that he wants to watch it with you and not in the basement by himself or who knows where! Don't turn your nose up in distaste—try to enjoy it or maybe even learn something. It could lead to a very erotic evening!

5. Go to an action-adventure movie with him, even though you'd rather see a touchy-feely bonding movie. You can always see a woman's movie by yourself or with one of your friends or sister. You never know, you may like thrillers. We know several married women who absolutely hated car-chasing movies and are now hooked on James Bond–Harrison Ford–Bruce Willis flicks.

6. Maybe your husband is into antique car shows or going to car dealerships on Sunday to test-drive sports cars. You and he both know he isn't going to buy anything, but he loves to look and drive, and this is his idea of fun. So indulge him! We know one hus-

band who liked to call real-estate brokers every week to show him mansions on Sundays even though he didn't have the money and had no plans to move. He liked to window-shop and wanted his wife to come along. It made no sense to her, but it made him feel so important to talk about acreage, backyards, and down payments, she figured who was she to deprive him of such pleasure. Men aren't crazy, they're just different from us. Don't you like to look in fashion magazines at $3,000 cocktail dresses you can't afford and will never buy?

7. If he asks to talk to you when you're on the phone or on the computer, don't say, "I'm busy" or "In a minute," unless it's a serious business matter. If not, get off quickly. Let him feel important. Make his day!

8. If your husband is an adventurer and you're not—he likes to discover new and interesting food at restaurants or visit the latest museum exhibition—don't hold him back. Pretend you're excited, too. Wouldn't you encourage a wide-eyed ten-year-old to experience and try new things? Why not do the same for your husband?

9. Try to do things around the house the way *he* wants it. If he likes the mail and his newspaper left on the table in the foyer, not on the kitchen table, leave it there. If he likes a certain bread served with dinner, put it on your grocery list. When you were single, you may not have cared about these things, but men feel more at home when domestic things are done a

certain way for them. For some men, details really matter!

10. Fill up the family car with gas before a big trip. Do something he usually does, like have the car washed. Replace his bar of soap or shampoo or toothpaste if you see it's getting skimpy. He will appreciate these little acts of kindness!

Will your husband leave you if you don't do these things? Probably not. But will he be happy? Probably not. He may come home late a lot or start finding excuses not to be home. Even if he's home a lot, a grumpy, dissatisfied partner is no fun to be around. So do all or some of the above or try to think of ways to make him happy and you will be happy, too.

It will be much easier to ask your husband to accompany you to things he has no interest in—an antique fair, a fur coat sale—if you have been a good sport, showed up for him once or twice, or done him a favor that week. So do it!

Rule #24: _____

He Can Say Anything About His Family but You Can't

You can choose your husband, but you can't choose his family. Some women are blessed with wonderful in-laws who welcome them into their families with open arms. Others are cursed with in-laws from hell—they think nobody is good enough for their son or they find fault with everything you do—and other difficult family members that can wreak havoc with your marriage. Life isn't fair!

The question becomes how do you love your husband while disliking his family and still keep your marriage intact? It's not easy, but it's definitely doable. Pretend you are studying diplomacy or public relations for college credit because that's exactly what it's going to take!

First and foremost, you must not talk badly about your in-laws or any other member of his family to your husband. If his family or any member of it is truly awful (or cheap or insensitive or tacky or whatever they are), trust us, he knows it! He may even criticize his family from time to time, but that's okay, it's *his* family. But he doesn't want to hear it from anyone, especially from you. Don't ever expect him to choose between you and his family, don't even put him in that position. If you say anything negative, he will either defend them, find fault with you, or tune out. So don't waste your time trying to get him to see your side. You will never get anywhere by telling your husband.

Does the following post dinner scenario sound familiar? On the car ride home from his mother's Christmas dinner, Debbie complained to her husband, Jeff, that his cousin Donna always puts her down. Jeff said he didn't know what she was talking about. "She asked me what I got for Christmas. I told her you bought me a stationary bicycle. You know what she said? She said, 'Are you sure you're going to use it? Why don't you just bike around the neighborhood?'"

"She wasn't putting you down. A lot of people buy exercise equipment and don't use it. Besides, why do you care what she thinks?" said Jeff.

"She never has anything good to say to me," said Debbie, tears in her eyes.

"You're being too sensitive. Just stop thinking about it," he said.

"Why do you always take her side? This isn't the first time. You're just like her! Mean!"

"You're crazy. This conversation is over!" said Jeff, turning on the radio so loud as to silence any further discussion.

Debbie felt hurt, alone, and sorry for herself, all because she said something negative about Jeff's family. She was looking for sympathy and got even more hurt. Another time, when she complained that his mother was giving unsolicited advice about how to feed, bathe, and dress their children, Jeff again took his mother's side. "She's just trying to be helpful."

A fight about his family would lead to marital spats that lasted for days. Fights of this nature are quite common among married couples. "My greatest aggravation with my husband is his family," says Sandi, who has been married two years. "He has two sisters, a brother, and a mother who live close by and are very needy. His family would spend every evening with us if we let them. Fortunately, my husband agrees that they are needy but he won't do anything about it. When we were first married, I spent a lot of energy being annoyed and angry with them and in turn annoyed and angry with my husband for not stepping in and fixing whatever was bothering me. As time went on, I realized that there was absolutely nothing I could do about them. You can't change your husband and you can't change your mother-in-law. So I just accept them and look the other way."

If you are tired of fighting with your husband about his family, we suggest you figure out some way to complain to a friend or find a therapist. When you are with your husband, talk only positively about his family or say nothing at all. When you are returning home from any event involving his family—a wedding, a dinner, whatever—try to find something positive to say, such as how great everyone looked, how wonderful the food was, how nice it was to see his parents again, anything you can think of without actually lying. At first, this will not be easy and you might feel less than genuine. But look at it this way. Everybody has a lower self who finds fault with other people and gossips, and a higher self who sees the good in everyone. We are just asking you to go to your higher self—for one car ride. We know how tempting it is to assassinate the character of a mean brother-in-law or an insensitive father-in-law on a long, boring car ride, but bite your tongue. Keep practicing talking nicely about them and it will become easier and more natural to do so.

We are not asking you to be best friends with his parents or siblings or to spend any extra time with them, but whenever you are thrown together, you should be cordial, warm, and generous in spirit. Out of respect for your husband, you should try to get along with them as much as possible. Remember to send a birthday card or gift, to wish them happy New Year, to call when someone is sick. Treat it like charity work. Most important, say nothing unkind. You will only hurt your husband, not his family. Be one of those people who only has good things to say about other people. Your husband will appreciate it and your marriage will be better for it.

Also remember not to get involved in family dynamics or disputes. Sometimes a newly married woman will call us to say that she doesn't like the way her husband treats his parents or vice versa. She wants to tell her husband that he should see his parents more often. "They're not going to be around forever," she'll remind him. Of course, her husband resents her interference and rightly so. They're *his* parents.

We tell her to stay out of it: None of your business. You weren't there when he was five or fifteen or maybe even twenty-five years old. You don't know how they treated your husband or why they are not as close as you would like, but it's not your job to dictate his behavior. Children need to be told what to do, not adults. Leave him alone.

So if you are the type to tell your husband to call his mother more often or to actually dial her number and put your husband on the phone, mind your own business and find something else to do with your time. Conversely, if your husband loaned his brother $5,000 five years ago and has yet to be repaid, don't tell your husband to have nothing to do with him until he sees the money. Just stay out of it. Your husband didn't marry you to play social director or judge and jury.

Whether he's too close to his family or not close enough, it is *his* family, and *his* choice. Remember this, and your family dynamics will be a lot smoother.

Make Him Feel Like He's the Most Important Person in Your Life

Let's say you're close to your sister and you talk to her almost every day. Before you met your husband, you rarely made a decision without consulting her. Now that you're married, it's easy to still call her first for advice, whether it's about what dress to wear to a wedding or a major career move.

But if you want to be happily married, consult your husband first. Make him feel like he's number one. Every husband wants to feel that *he's* your best friend, your life partner, your soul mate. So even if you are more comfortable confiding in your sister, make sure you take the time to ask your husband for his opinion first. You must feed his ego. Remember, men like to solve problems and feel good when they can rescue you or at least steer you in the right direction.

Marcy and her older sister, Nancy, have been close since birth. Marcy consulted Nancy about everything from what lipstick shade to wear to where to go on her honeymoon. When Marcy wanted to redo her master bedroom, she called Nancy, who had just done hers, for advice. Then she called her husband, Peter, at work and told him she wanted to buy the same bedspread and furniture Nancy had. Peter was furious. He would have liked Marcy to talk to *him* first about his taste in redoing such an important room, even though he didn't know anything about fabrics and had no preference for Formica or wood.

"But you don't know anything about decorating and Nancy just redid her bedroom," said Marcy, surprised by his reaction.

"I would have looked at some furniture catalogs and talked to my friends. Isn't there anything you can do without Nancy's seal of approval?" Peter fumed.

The conversation turned into a big argument about how decisions should be made and how money should be spent. "We're married a year now and you're still acting and spending like a single person!" screamed Peter.

"You didn't consult me when you bought your sports car!" Marcy shouted.

"Just go out and redo the bedroom with Nancy, your *significant other*," he shot back.

The argument could have been avoided if Marcy had simply consulted Peter first and let him feel included by allowing him to shop around and read decorating magazines. She should have included him, and listened as he analyzed the pros and cons of venetian blinds. She could have let Peter feel like it was *their* decision, not her sister's. She would have still been able to order the bedroom set Nancy had; there was just no need to let Peter know that her sister's recommendation mattered so much.

Being happily married means being a little bit of a diplomat. No man likes to feel like a rubber stamp, okay-ing whatever decisions you make with your sister, mother, or best friend. By all means, continue to talk to everybody else, but consult your husband first. Ask him about the kitchen, ask him what dress you should wear to the wedding, or which treadmill to buy. He will feel flattered and you can still do whatever's good for you.

Let's say you have a best friend whom you consult about everything from work issues to sex. This friend literally keeps you alive during bad times and you do the same for her. But if you don't want your husband to be jealous of the closeness you share with her, try to be discreet about exactly how influential she is.

If your husband finds your best friend's hold over you annoying or intrusive, try not to be on the phone with her when he is at home. Discuss your interactions sparingly. Do not flaunt her name in conversations—don't tell him you want to go to *x* restaurant because Mindy said it was fabulous. Don't tell him that you want to go to Aruba because Mindy was just there. Don't tell him you don't want to have a third child because Mindy has two and says three is too much work. Be sensitive. No man wants his next vacation spot or dynasty to be determined by someone else. If he likes Mindy you can mention her name once in a while, but just in passing, not in terms of any important decisions. But if he doesn't like Mindy because he thinks she's a bad influence—she spends too much money, smokes or drinks too much, has cheated on her husband—do not mention her at all.

Men simply do not understand the importance of female bonding, even if you try to explain it to them. They believe a husband and wife should be able to figure everything out for themselves—privately. That's because, unlike women, most men do not call their best friends every day to make decisions. There's a joke that all a man knows about his best friend of twenty-five years is his first name, age, if he's a good basketball player, and what he does for a living. A woman, on the other hand, will strike up a conversation with another woman at the beauty parlor and know her astrological sign, the names of all her children and baby-sitter, and what car she drives within five minutes. With a best friend, she will know how much they pay their nanny and how often they fight and what about without blinking an eye—facts a man might never tell the best man at his wedding.

Indeed, if your husband knew how much you told your friends about your private life, he would be shocked and upset. But if you are the kind of person who needs to share intimate details of your life with a best friend or needs her advice to make good decisions, we understand and think it's perfectly okay. Just make sure you don't let your husband know exactly how important she is.

If he asks, "So how many times did you talk to Mindy today?" or "Let me guess, does Mindy also have those shoes?" just say you haven't spoken to Mindy in a while. (He will think you mean a few days, we know you mean a few hours.) And then change the subject. Ask him about work.

Here's another tip to make your husband feel like he's numero uno, especially if you have a close sibling or best friend. You are having a riveting conversation with your sibling or a friend who is telling you all about her steamy date. Your husband comes home and wants to talk about plans for the weekend. You don't want to be rude, but you don't want to stop what you are doing either. Stop what you are doing. Call your friend back. It's worth the delayed gratification to make your husband feel he's first. How would you like it if you came home and your husband wouldn't look up from his newspaper to talk to you? Try to be considerate. (You can talk to your sister or friend later on or the next day.) Remember, friends come and go, but hopefully your husband will be around for a long time, so make him feel important!

Rule #26: _____

Listen to His Advice and Try to Appreciate It

Most men like to fix things even when they're not broken. They're problem-solvers. Women don't necessarily want their problems solved, they just want to air their feelings, to be heard. So when your husband gives you unsolicited advice, don't think he is insinuating that you don't know what you're doing. It has nothing to do with your competency, he's just following his problem-solving nature.

Sally does career counseling from home. Her business has skyrocketed primarily because she lets clients call her with work issues and quick questions at all hours of the day. One evening as she was cooking dinner and the kids were playing with the dog, a client called and asked, "Do you have a second? I just have one question and it can't wait until tomorrow. I'm catching a plane in five minutes for a job interview in Boston."

"Sure, as long as you don't mind the commotion. We're just about to eat dinner," said Sally. She put her hand over the receiver and told her kids to be quiet. The client didn't mind at all.

Her husband Jeff had just walked in the door and over-heard the conversation. After Sally answered the client's question and hung up the phone, she kissed Jeff hello, and said, "Gosh, it's always crazy around here. The kids, the dog, the phone . . ."

"Can I make a suggestion?" asked Jeff. "Why did you have to take that call? Is that any way to run a business with screaming kids and pots rattling in the background? Couldn't you have told her to call back in an hour?"

Sally was furious. If anything, she was looking for a lit-tle praise about how much she juggles in a day. She didn't want career advice. She knew the reason her new business was successful was because clients could call with emer-gency questions at odd hours. For Jeff to insinuate she didn't know what she was doing was infuriating.

"She was catching a plane and needed to talk to me now. She didn't mind the background noise, why do you? Why don't you stick to accounting?" she screamed. Of course, she could have said, "Thanks, but I'm handling everything just fine. Tell me about your day." That would have not hurt Jeff's feelings and would have diffused any tension.

Instead, they argued for hours. Sally complained that Jeff always had a better way to do everything even though she never asked him for it. Jeff said she was being too sen-sitive. Sally is not alone. Many women complain that their husbands are always trying to control or fix them or offer unsolicited advice when they are doing just fine, thank you. These women get insulted—they feel their competency is being questioned—and they end up screaming at their husbands, which only makes matters worse.

Here are two more examples: Mary travels constantly as a book publicist and has never missed a flight. Yet her husband Ben always reminds her to leave for the airport earlier. It makes him feel important that he's having a say in her schedule. She gets so irritated by his interference that she ends up lying about her flight times and giving him a cold kiss good-bye.

Joan, a magazine writer, is the first to admit she's a slob. Her desk is always messy, her closets are cluttered, her drawers won't close and her appointment books are illegible, yet she has never missed a doctor's appointment, a deadline, a PTA meeting, never forgotten a friend or relative's birthday or lost her keys. Her husband, Steve, an MBA grad, is always trying to organize her. He has bought her a fancy Filofax every Christmas for the last twelve years, despite the fact that they sit in her closet unused. She has a method that works for her, even though no one else can fathom her system. Yet Steve is intent on reforming her. When he makes a comment about being afraid to put anything on her desk because it might get lost, she wants to scream! Instead she gets so hurt that she won't speak to him for a few hours.

If you feel like screaming or sulking every time your husband tells you how to run your life, realize that he's not attacking you. Believe it or not, he's just trying to be helpful. It makes him feel important to put his two cents in. Try to understand his point of view. Women used to need a man for everything from programming a VCR to paying taxes. Now women are so self-sufficient that they don't need a man to run a business or invest in the stock market. Men are feeling a little insecure about that, so they try to get involved any way they can.

Understanding that, the next time your husband gives you advice you didn't ask for and probably won't use, just listen politely and say, "Thank you. That's a good idea," and then do what you were going to do anyway (unless he really does have a better idea).

Don't be insulted, offended, or turn the comment into a big argument. Be flattered that he wants to help you. A lot of wives complain that their husbands ignore them. Be grateful you're not one of them.

Rule #27: —————————————————————

Don't Try to Do It All

The modern married woman is a harried woman. She has a big juggling act to do—career, kids, PTA, housework, exercise, groceries, shopping, maintaining friendships, planning vacations, and so on. If you try to do it all, you will become a wreck.

If you work too much, your husband and kids will suffer. If you spend too much time on housework, your looks will suffer. If you run around with big to-do lists every day and never get any rest, you will be too tired to exercise or have sex or everything else for that matter. Don't try to be a perfectionist. Better that you nap for thirty minutes and leave a few chores undone than have a spotless house and be angry and irritable all the time.

We believe in getting extra help—as much help as you can afford and your husband is willing to go along with—and not feeling guilty about it, either. Just tell yourself, "I deserve it," and eventually you will believe it.

Note: If you feel you deserve *everything*—you don't

work, you have no problem paying other people to take care of your kids or do errands and chores, and you spend money like water (you have five pairs of the same shoes because you couldn't decide which color)—skip this chapter. This chapter is for women who try to do too much, act like martyrs trying to handle everything, who tend to be stingy with money, and must be told by good friends that they deserve the cleaning lady, a new dress, a haircut, and baby-sitter. You know who you are.

If you grew up with parents from the Depression era who didn't believe in eating out or even ordering in ("It's cheaper to eat at home"), taxis ("Why can't you take a bus or walk? What's your hurry?"), joining a gym ("Just walk up and down the stairs"), ordering from catalogs ("How can you buy something without trying it on first? Why pay extra for delivery?"), hiring a cleaning lady ("Mopping the floor is good exercise"), or any other modern convenience, you will find this rule hard to follow. You will feel guilty, you will feel like you are overindulging, wasting money, and acting like a princess.

Try to remember that your mother didn't have a fast-track career with all its pressures and crazy hours. Maybe she didn't work at all, so she had the time and energy to raise children and clean the house. Don't compare yourself to your mother. Don't let her make you feel guilty for taking care of yourself, especially if she is the type to come to your house and ask, "Why do you need a cleaning lady every week? Twice a month isn't enough? The house isn't that big." Don't argue with her, but don't listen to her either. Remember, she's probably coming from another era. In your mother's day, very often her mother lived upstairs or across the street and helped her out with the house-work. That is just not the case today. If you try to do it all you will lose your strength and sanity. You need to conserve your energy for yourself, your family, and your work.

Here are ten suggestions to make your life easier:

1. Find a way to get a cleaning lady or college student to help you around the house. Whether it's once a week or twice a month, just do it. Living in a dirty house with dust and clutter and piles of laundry is depressing, unhealthy, and bad for your marriage. If your husband doesn't want to spend the money, negotiate with him. Say you want it for your birthday, or try to save money somewhere else. Whatever you do, don't skimp on household help. Elsewhere in this book we have told you your husband is always right, but in this case he's not. If you try to clean and work and be a wife and a mother who reads to her children every night, you will have a nervous breakdown, which is more expensive when you add up psychiatrists' fees! Don't be penny wise and pound foolish.

2. Have groceries and anything else delivered. Call your local supermarkets, cleaners, drugstores and hardware stores and see if they deliver. Some women fax, call, or e-mail their shopping list to supermarkets every week and pay a few extra dollars for the luxury of not having to go to the store. Sometimes this service is free, especially in large cities, so look into it! Some cities have on-line companies that provide the same service. Shopping is exhausting and time-consuming, so if you can have groceries and other

items delivered, do it. Speaking of food, don't feel you have to cook a five-course meal from scratch every night. If your husband likes home-cooked meals, you can make the main course (chicken, fish, etc.) and order in interesting side dishes like lasagna or mashed potatoes that require extra pots or are too time-consuming to cook.

3. Try to order clothes, supplies, toys, gifts, and anything else you can on-line or by catalog. If you are the kind of person who resists change and new technology, you might think shopping by computer or mail is for MIT grads, not you, but try it and see how easy it is. Why go to stores and deal with parking and long lines when you can sit at your desk and order by phone? Yes, you may have to return some things because they don't look or fit the way you thought they would, but you have to return things to stores, too. Shopping in person can be draining and hectic, so ordering at home is just another way to conserve energy.

4. If you have no time to go to the gym, buy a treadmill, stationary bicycle, floor mat, weights, or some form of exercise equipment and/or exercise videos and work out at home. Don't think, "I don't have time to go to the gym so I'll do nothing." Surely you can find twenty or thirty minutes at home to do *something*. Having equipment at home compels you to exercise when you can't find a sitter to watch your kids or the weather is too bad to leave the house to go to the gym. You have no excuse if you have equipment at home! You can always watch TV or talk on the

phone while exercising so you won't feel you're wasting time. Exercise keeps you firm, is nature's antidepressant, and gives you energy, so set aside at least twenty minutes three times a week to move your muscles.

5. Hire a baby-sitter. Don't be so attached and protective of your children—or just plain frugal—that you refuse to hire a baby-sitter to go out with your husband on Saturday night or just to go out with your friends on a weeknight. Don't think, "She won't know how to handle the kids. What if they cry? What if they don't eat?" Your kids will be fine without you. In fact, it is healthy for them—and healthy for you—to spend time apart so they can gain independence. Don't be the kind of overly doting mother who won't separate, who takes the kids on every errand, every vacation, who only goes to parties where kids are allowed and ruins her husband's social life by refusing to double with couples or do any adult-only activities. Take a cell phone with you and check up on your kids every hour if you must, but go!

6. Don't make work your whole life. It's great to be ambitious, but you have to know when to stop, when to say, "how important is it?" Unless you absolutely have to, don't bring work home and ignore your husband and kids on evenings and weekends. Don't miss your son's Little League game because of work. Try to get as much done as you can in the office. How? Skip long nonessential business lunches. Delegate. Prioritize. Don't let coworkers or clients waste your time and energy with anything over and beyond your

work projects, such as gossip and politics. Remember that work is a part of your life, not your whole life. Workaholism inevitably takes its toll on your health, your looks, your family, and you end up stressed-out, burned-out, and sick, which is more costly in the long run. The extra money and status are not worth a crazy, unbalanced life.

7. Leave your answering machine on at work and home. Another great way to save time and energy is to screen your calls. Why answer every solicitation call or wrong number? Answering every call can take hours out of your day, and leave you feeling fatigued and depressed yourself. Don't try to be Mother Teresa. You can't help everyone. Trust that these people will find other people to call if you're not around. Your priority is your mental health, your husband, and family. If you try to be Dear Abby to everyone in your life you will have nothing left to give to yourself, your husband, kids, and career, which are your top priorities. If you must talk to a few close friends, at least try to end the conversation after ten to fifteen minutes. Just say you wish you could stay on the phone longer but are on the way out or must get back to whatever you were doing. Setting boundaries will be difficult for you if you are used to being everything and doing everything for everyone, but it will get easier with practice and you will have added hours to your day.

8. Practice saying no. You do not have to bake cookies for every holiday your kids have at school, you do not have to be Class Mother, you do not have to give

money to every charity that knocks on your door, you do not have to say yes to every play date or sleepover or toy your kids demand, and you do not have to return every phone call you receive. If you are finding yourself exhausted all the time, perhaps it's because you are saying yes to everything. Try saying no sometimes and you'll find that the rest of the world will adjust just fine.

9. Do not try to be a Martha Stewart clone, be yourself. If you compare your cooking, your drapes, your serving utensils, and your flower arrangements to experts, TV shows, magazine spreads, and those of more homemaker-type friends, you will inevitably end up feeling inadequate. If you work and raise children, your house need not look like a magazine cover. Lower your expectations, otherwise you will never be happy with anything you do. If your house is clean and there is fresh food in the refrigerator and furniture you like in your house, paintings and photos on the walls, and you are not embarrassed to have people over, you are doing just fine.

10. Follow the easy plan. Whenever you have a choice, do whatever's less stressful no matter what other people think. Sometimes it's less stressful to spend a week's vacation time at home relaxing, catching up on rest, reading, and playing with the kids than packing everyone up to go skiing in Colorado or sunning in Puerto Rico. Assuming your husband and you are in agreement on staying home, don't force yourself to go on a fancy vacation because you'd be mortified to tell anyone you didn't go anywhere. Don't go to Eu-

rope just to impress your friends and neighbors if in fact taking any trip will be exhausting and what you really need and want is rest. Some women feel that between packing and flying and running around sightseeing—not to mention the errands and piles of mail and telephone messages to be dealt with when they get home—they are exhausted by vacations and need a week to recover. If this is how you feel, take the easy way out. Don't go places or do things just to impress other people or because it sounds good. Just do what's good for you. We are not saying you will never have an exciting vacation again, but if you are feeling burned-out and have young children, save it for another year.

Rule #28: ────────────────────

Have a Date Night

Whether or not you have children (but this is even more crucial if you do), you must keep the romance going by reserving one night alone with your husband, preferably Saturday night. It doesn't matter if you rent a video and order in or go to a restaurant and movie. The point is to do whatever it takes so that it's just the two of you. Get a baby-sitter or send the kids over to grandma's house. You need one night a week without diapers, whining, phone calls, beepers, the dishwasher going, crises from family, friends, business associates, clients. You're unavailable . . . what a concept!

Don't think, "But my children need me!" Think, "My children need me to maintain a relationship with their father." Don't add up the cost of going out to dinner—the baby-sitter, the restaurant, the overpriced drinks and dessert, the parking, the movie tickets. Don't think it's cheaper to eat at home. It *is* cheaper to eat at home, but you simply must have a break from the routine. It's money well spent if it makes you and your husband feel alive, like you're dating.

It doesn't matter if you have to do all the planning, as long as somebody does it. Don't stand on ceremony. Whatever it takes.

Also, if you're usually tired on Saturdays—and who isn't that has kids and/or a full-time job?—take a nap or lie down for twenty minutes in the afternoon so you can stay up at night. Wear what you think he would like you to wear. If he likes short skirts, high heels, and hoop earrings, wear that even if you feel more comfortable in a pantsuit and loafers. Make an effort to look better than you usually do Sunday through Friday. Wash your hair, put on mascara, try a new lipstick color, dab a little more perfume on, wear a new, exciting shirt. You know that shirt that you're always saving for a special occasion? A daytime wedding or important business lunch, but not for your husband? Well, on Saturday nights your husband *is* the special occasion. Wear it!

What to talk about? Don't use the evening to complain about your job, the kids, finances, what needs to be done around the house. We know how you feel—he's your hostage for the evening and this is a perfect opportunity to go over your laundry list of grievances and/or things to be done. Save it for Sunday afternoon. On Saturday nights, keep it light. Try to listen to him. Smile. Pretend you're dating him all over again. Plan to have sex. Let that be the topping on a perfectly romantic evening.

We have found that marriages where the wives do not take date night and sex seriously have less passion and fun. The couple starts to act like roommates, not lovers, and this can go on for months, sometimes years.

Now what if you like to go out and your husband is a homebody? Some wives have found that if they make all the arrangements, their husbands happily join in. Whereas if they wait for their husbands to suggest going out, they never do. Do whatever you have to do to make sure date night happens.

But if your husband would really rather eat at home and watch a movie on TV, don't nag him to go out; you can still make it special.

Here are ten tips for a romantic evening at home:

1. Order in a gourmet dinner, but don't use cartons or paper plates, use the real stuff.
2. Eat in your lingerie.
3. Take out the rarely used candlesticks you got as a wedding gift and dim the lights.
4. Put on a romantic CD.
5. Turn off the phones.
6. Rent a sexy video.
7. Give him a backrub.
8. Be playful—tell him you're his slave/sex toy for the night.
9. Don't talk about anything negative or serious.
10. Pretend you're auditioning for a toothpaste commercial. Smile!

Rule #29:

Rules for Sex

When it comes to sex in a marriage, husbands rule the roost. Whether you like it or not or think it's right or fair, your husband determines your sex life. Whether your husband wants it all the time or is not that interested in sex, you will be happiest if you adjust yourself accordingly. So don't turn your husband down repeatedly if he wants sex every night even if you're a morning person, and don't force sex on a man who wants to watch Larry King or read a book after dinner. Go with the flow, whatever that is in your marriage. We have seen time and again that in this area, it is best for your husband to set the tone.

For example Keith enjoyed a wild sex life before settling down with his wife, Maria. He expected more of the same as a married man, which his wife found exhausting. She constantly came up with excuses. She was either tired or had PMS or the kids were draining. Keith got angry every time. "You're always tired. Your period is either coming, here, or going. You have it thirty days a month," he screamed. "We're just roommates if we don't have more sex!" He also reminded Maria how exciting his sex life was before he married her.

After seeing how unhappy Keith was and finding that her marriage had become passionless, Maria consulted us and decided to make her sex life a priority. "He either wants to have sex with you or his 38-D secretary. Be flattered he wants to have it with you! Make the effort. A man like Keith wants sex more than anything else. He works hard, pays bills, and helps with the kids. Sex is fun for him, it's his candy, his break. Don't take that away from him," we explained.

We told her to act as if she was dating her husband all over again and experiment with what would make him happy sexually (as long as she didn't find it offensive), to cut down on other activities so she wasn't so tired when he came home, to stop neglecting her sex life because of her kids (get a baby-sitter), to stop rolling her eyes when he rented X-rated videos, and to even occasionally resort to pretending she enjoyed sex even when she would rather be watching TV. Maria followed our advice and Keith was thrilled. Maria had to admit that cuddling before and after sex made her feel close to her husband, so it was worth the extra effort.

On the other hand some women want more sex than their husbands and don't know what to do about this problem. For example, Janice contacted us about her frustration with her husband, Michael, a stockbroker who often came home late from work and showed little interest in sex—once or twice a month on a Saturday night was enough for him. When he came home, he typically gave her a hug and a kiss and asked about her day, and then he went straight to the den to read newspapers or check stocks on his computer. Taking a detour into the bedroom for a quickie somehow never crossed his serious, cerebral mind.

"Michael gets off on the Dow Jones," Janice complained to anyone who would listen. Rather than accept his low sex drive, Janice threw tantrums and put pressure on him to make love. Sometimes she was nice about it, greeting him at the door with sexy negligees. At other times she screamed at him, demanding to know what was wrong with him, with her, with their sex life, and threatening to call a sex therapist for a session. Nothing seemed to work, he only wanted sex once or twice a month. Even when Michael gave in to her demands to have sex more often, Janice felt embarrassed and ashamed, like she was begging.

In every other way, Janice was happy with Michael and would never think of divorcing him. He was extremely romantic and affectionate, and a devoted husband and father. It was only his lack of interest in sex that bothered her.

When we asked about their sex life while dating, Janice admitted that it was only once a week, but she didn't really think about it that much because she was caught up in the excitement of the courtship. He was very romantic and often brought her flowers on dates. She didn't notice the lack of sex or she thought that he was being polite about not trying to end up in bed every time he saw her. She also assumed that their sex life would change when they got married and became angry and demanding when it didn't.

We told her that unfortunately some men have low sex drives and some men put all their sexual energy into work or sports and that she would have to accept that Michael was one of them. We said that it would be okay for her to gently initiate sex once in a while, but no screaming fits and threats. We also suggested she compliment his performance instead of harping on how infrequently they had sex. After six months of trying our plan, she said she felt better. Even though the sex was not much more frequent than before, she stopped expecting it to change and was more accepting that you don't get everything in a husband. And once Michael realized that Janice was satisfied with his performance, he relaxed considerably. She found that Michael did not mind his wife's sexual advances, except when she did it in anger, and was actually flattered by the attention and happy to have sex with her at those times. Their sex life was never three times a week, but it was more enjoyable than before.

A word about *Playboy* and *Penthouse,* X-rated videos and sex toys. Don't hassle your husband about subscribing to these magazines, renting adult movies, buying gadgets, or even occasionally going to bachelor parties held at topless clubs. You can jokingly say, "You can look but don't touch!" A man's fascination with nudity is not a reflection of his love for you. It's just entertainment for him, much like window-shopping at Bergdorf's may be for you. You don't have to understand *why* they like it. Just don't show any disdain or prohibit them from indulging in this pleasure. Men don't necessarily understand women's obsession with handbags and shoes or watching fashion shows on the E! channel. How would you like it if they said "No more E! channel!" It's not about understanding why, but about live and let live and allowing your husband to have fun. If you think of it this way, you will realize there is no harm in letting him look at a bare-chested woman in a magazine from time to time.

Rule #30: _____

Rules for Pregnancy

A baby can be the most amazing gift in the entire world, but no matter how wanted a pregnancy is, it always has an effect on your relationship. Going into pregnancy with your eyes open will help you to manage these changes. The first decision you must face is whether you should get pregnant.

If your relationship is rocky, do not get pregnant to bring your husband closer. You should be close *before* you have a baby. Babies are very demanding—taking care of them puts *more* stress on a marriage, not less. Husbands and wives who are exhausted from diaper changes, feedings, and sleepless nights often say mean things to each other that they would never say otherwise ("When's the last time you changed his diaper? In the delivery room?") Unless your marriage is solid, do not bring a child into the picture. Before you get pregnant, make sure that the baby is a by-product of your love, not a hidden agenda.

Similarly, don't get pregnant to get your boyfriend to

marry you or to keep your husband from leaving you. This is a terrible reason to bring a child into the world. A child should not be used as a pawn to settle your marital squabbles or cement your relationship. Besides, bad motives always backfire. Married men walk out on pregnant women all the time—some leave the delivery room to go to the bathroom and never come back. Having a baby is no guarantee of *anything*. Bringing a child into a marriage should be a mutual decision, so try to come to a consensus before proceeding.

If you do decide to get pregnant, the timing can be crucial. Don't rush. Pregnancy is a life-changing adjustment in any marriage. So unless you have a reason to have a baby immediately—your age—we suggest being married a full year before you try to get pregnant. There are several reasons to wait. First and foremost, make sure you can be happy together for a whole year, not up and down and on the verge of divorce every other week.

Waiting a year also gives the two of you precious time together that you won't have again for at least eighteen years—a year of sipping cappuccinos in a romantic café without having to rush home to the baby-sitter, of traveling unencumbered by a diaper bag and stroller, of having an intelligent conversation and/or sex without being interrupted by baby feedings, not to mention a year of uninterrupted sleep. And that's the least of it. Pregnancies can be extremely complicated and difficult—some women throw up every day and are so sick that they are on bedrest or even hospitalized. Why spend your "honeymoon" first year like that?

Now that you are pregnant, how should you behave?

You can spend your whole pregnancy complaining about every ache and pain—your swollen feet, your sore back, your stiff neck—and calling your husband at work every time you discover a new ailment so that he is forced to endure the worst of your pregnancy with you. Why should you suffer alone? You can talk incessantly about Lamaze and layettes and quote *What to Expect When You're Expecting* when he comes home. You can lie in bed for nine months eating potato chips and ice cream and watching soap operas, wear oversize sweatshirts and your husband's pajamas and look like a truck.

Or you can be pregnant with style. Instead of torturing your husband, you can complain to your mother or girl-friends who've been pregnant and know what you are going through and can truly empathize. If you are able, you should work for as long as possible so that your mind isn't on your stomach size twenty-four–seven. The nine months won't feel like nine years if you are busy being productive, not lying in bed with the remote control.

If you are physically able, you should exercise and eat healthy foods so that you look like a woman during and after your pregnancy. Think Cindy Crawford. You do not have to dress like a bum for nine months. There are many stores that carry fashionable pregnancy clothes at reason-able prices so you don't have to be ashamed to leave the house. Or try borrowing from a fashionable friend who has children.

Don't force your husband to be involved in every aspect of your pregnancy unless he wants to be. There are some men who go to every doctor's visit, never miss a Lamaze class, practice breathing with their wives at home, think *they* are having hormone swings and feel nauseous too, gain twenty-five pounds along with their wives, and read pregnancy books with them at night. If your husband is not one of them, don't try to guilt-trip him into it. When you meet other women who tell you how involved their husbands are, don't complain to your husband. Don't say, "Andrea's husband goes with her to every doctor's visit, why can't you?"

A better idea is to try to include him in the *fun* parts of pregnancy—letting him know when the baby is kicking, framing a photo of the sonogram for his desk, and going over baby names. But don't push *too* hard. He'll be a daddy soon enough!

Rule #31: _____

Don't Complain About the Kids

It's been one of those days. Your three-year-old is covered in mud and refuses to take a bath. Your five-year-old won't eat anything that's first ingredient isn't sugar and it always ends up on his shirt. Both don't let you talk on the phone for more than five minutes without interrupting. You want to pull your hair out! You can't wait until your husband comes home so you can go into exquisite detail over everything *his* kids did wrong today. We know how you feel, we've all had those days.

May we suggest you call a friend with children instead and tell her how hard your day was? She will be better able to relate to your tale of woe and maybe even help you laugh about it. Of course, nothing is wrong with telling your husband that the kids were acting up, but if you daily dish up every mishap, every Dennis the Menace caper, at some point (trust us!), he will stop commiserating with you and start to think you are simply *incompetent*.

We know mothers who call their husbands at work

every time their child doesn't finish dinner or throws a tantrum. They get hysterical over everything from potty training to broken vases to bad behavior at recess. We know one woman who called her husband at work because their five-year-old daughter was crying over a canceled play date. Her husband, who oversees thirty-five employees at an accounting firm and was in the middle of a meeting when his wife called, didn't know what to say. "Why don't you take her out for ice cream?" What can a husband possibly say or do? We know another woman who called her husband to say she was concerned that their six-year-old son always sat at the end, not the center, of the table at barbecues and birthday parties. Was he going to be a loner, was something wrong with him? Your husband doesn't need to hear this on a busy day.

These overly insecure mothers want their husbands to drop everything and help them through the latest crisis. Now, a new father might jump every time his wife calls, but if she constantly behaves hysterically, he will eventually tire of it and secretly think she doesn't know what she's doing. He may start to think, "My mother raised four children without my father's help, what's wrong with her?" He may start to worry while he's at work, "Can she really handle kids?" If you are constantly complaining about your kids, your husband may eventually start to question everything you do and make you feel worse. It may open a Pandora's box between the two of you. He may start asking a lot of questions, such as, "Are you sure that sweater is warm enough? It's really cold outside" or "Did you check the dosage with the pediatrician, that looks like a helluva lot of medicine for a two-year-old."

He might start questioning whether you are spending enough time with your children and feeding them all the right food groups. He may look bewildered every time you raise your voice or scold your child (even when the child deserves to be scolded) as if there is something wrong with *you!* He may suggest you take parenting classes or recommend a book on the subject. You will feel judged, unsupported and diminished. Trust us, if you let your husband constantly see how your kids upset you, he may be compassionate for a while, but then he will become your biggest critic, the resident backseat driver.

Now you might argue that the reason you like to share these kids issues with him is so that you bond with your husband, so that you feel you are raising your children together. If you want to bond with your husband as parents, may we suggest you tell him some positive things about your kids—Johnny brushed his teeth by himself today, Jane wrote her name for the first time, Brittany is saying please and thank you. He will appreciate happy news and think you are doing a good job. If you want to complain or vent or get sympathy, you are better off talking to your friends.

Around your husband, try to act and feel confident about your parenting skills. For example, don't ask your husband, "Do you think I should give Tommy a time-out for hitting Stacey?" Instead, just make the rules and stick to them. If you constantly seek your husband's help with parenting, he will think you are insecure and weak-willed. Don't show that you need your husband's approval. Just fake it until you make it. Instead of looking and acting like a harried, overwhelmed mother who lets her kids run amok, pretend you are the CEO of a company. Your house is the company, your kids are your employees, and you are running a tight ship. You will not accept insubordination. Make the rules for meals, bathing, bedtime, time-out and stick to them. Act confident, don't act flustered or back down easily. Kids will try to see what they can get away with, they will test you, so don't give in. The more structure you give your kids, the more they will respect you. Kids love boundaries and right and wrong, even though they say they don't and rebel against rules. If you act like you're in charge, you will have less to complain about to your husband and he will respect you and won't feel that he has to worry while he's at work.

After struggling for a couple of years raising two sons and complaining to her husband about how difficult they were, Sarah realized that the more she complained, the more judgmental and less sympathetic her husband became. "He worked twelve-hour days at a merger and acquisition firm. All he wanted was some peace and quiet in the morning and at night before and after work. But all I did was complain about the kids and try to involve him in every detail. When I stopped complaining and started to run the house like the army—with bathtimes and bedtimes and mealtimes and time-outs, not idle threats—my husband started to relax and appreciate me. He had one less thing to worry about."

A husband will respect a wife who seems to have everything under control, including homework, medical and school forms. Look at it this way: If your husband came home every day with another disaster story about work, looking disheveled with papers falling out of his briefcase, you might think he was incompetent. The same applies in reverse. Most husbands want to come home from a stressful workday to peace and quiet, a clean, organized house with kids who are well behaved. Let them.

Here's one more piece of advice, which we are sure that new moms in new neighborhoods or moms who recently stopped working will appreciate. Have you ever told your husband how hard it is to make friends with other mothers in the neighborhood? Did he say, "That's rough . . . you must be very lonely" and show sympathy? We doubt it. The husbands we know will say something like, "Well, maybe you should try harder, have you knocked on doors, asked anyone for lunch or a play date, are you going to the playground where the other mothers are? You can't just sit at home and expect women to find you."

Men don't understand that making friends with mothers in a new neighborhood is not that different from making friends in high school—there are established cliques and inner circles you just can't break into; these women either like you or they don't; if you ask a mother to have lunch or make a play date and she says "I'll think about it" and never calls you, you can feel hurt; that it's always best for a mother and child to want to be friends with you and your child, that *The Rules* still apply. On the other hand, the new mom who wants to be your friend, who asks *you* to lunch, will probably be your friend for life or until your toddler goes to college. She'll be the one who asks if you need anything at the grocery store since she is going or if you want her to watch your kid for an hour so you can do errands.

Men don't get this. They don't think there should be rules for dating or marriage, much less making friends and play dates, but there are. If you try to explain the politics of making friends and play dates in a new neighborhood to your husband, you will probably be misunderstood. Call a girlfriend.

Rule #32: _____

Keep It to Yourself

1. What a hunk your new boss is—do you want to hear how gorgeous his coworker is?
2. Your sexual fantasies that have nothing to do with him—no explanation needed here.
3. How gorgeous you think a certain actor is, especially if your husband doesn't look anything like that actor. For example, if you're watching a movie and he says, "So you think he's cute?," tone down your true feelings. If your husband is short, and the guy on the screen is six foot six, say, "Tall men are kind of scary!"
4. The extramarital affair your friend is having—it'll make him nervous.
5. The mess (and extra work for you) your husband creates every time he offers to make you dinner or bathe your three-year-old. That's right. Pretend you don't notice the smoke in the kitchen and the flood in the bathroom.
6. The telephone messages for you he forgets to take down—they called again, didn't they?

7. How *not in the mood* you are to make love.
8. The fact that he is incapable of putting dishes in the sink—he does help out in other ways.
9. The dysfunctional way he folds the laundry—at least he's folding it!
10. How you *really* feel about his family or friends—there's nothing he can do about his family, and he chose his friends for a reason.

Rule #33: _____

Don't Expect Applause
for Doing Chores

Even in this age of dual-career couples, most of the housework and kids' work falls on the wife/mother (unless you have one of those rare househusband-types).

If you are like most married women, you buy the groceries, you cook, you clip coupons and wait for sales to buy winter coats, you do the laundry and vacuuming, you make the beds, you call the baby-sitter, you make the restaurant reservations, and you call the travel agent to plan vacations. And your husband doesn't walk around the house thanking you for each and every task. You feel taken for granted. (Doesn't he notice that you've never run out of milk and bananas for his cereal in eight years? Does he realize how many times you've checked the milk cartons' expiration dates to make sure it's not sour?)

In a bad moment, you may scream, "Do you think this house looks like this by magic? Who do you think made the beds and put away the dishes? Mary Poppins? I do everything around here. Why can't you say thank you once in a while?"

Your husband will probably look bewildered—"What are you talking about?"—or feel guilty and mumble, "I do appreciate everything you do." But because you demanded that he be appreciative, you don't feel any better. Demanding appreciation is never the way to get it. Realize that your husband notices everything you do and may even brag to his friends or parents about how organized you are. He probably told you once—"Thanks for cooking, cleaning," and he feels that should last for twenty years. He doesn't feel the need to say it every time you cook dinner or pick up the dry cleaning, just as he doesn't feel he needs to thank every employee who comes to work on time. After all, you don't thank him every time he goes to work or takes out the garbage.

You, on the other hand, wouldn't mind recognition morning, noon and night. Unfortunately, you only hear about it when there's a problem, which is even more infuriating. "I think you shrank my shirt" or "We're out of ketchup." That's because men are problem-solvers. They notice problems, not good work. They notice what's wrong, not what's right. Our motto: don't expect applause and you won't be disappointed. The reason you should make the beds and buy groceries is because it's the right thing to do and it makes you feel good to have a clean, orderly house. You must pat yourself on the back for doing these things, especially if no one else does. (There's a reason they call it thankless work!)

Jane and Jimmy were having a housewarming party. Jane decided to have all the food catered because cooking wasn't her strong suit and she had plenty of other things to do—decorating the house, cleaning, sending sixty invitations, buying soda and paper goods. It took her a month to organize the party. Jimmy didn't say one word about all the work she had done. After the party was over, she said, "Gosh, that was so much work. I'm exhausted."

"What work? All the food was catered!" he replied. Jane was furious and a fight ensued. "What work? What about invitations for sixty people and cleaning the house and the flower arrangements? There's more to a party than food!"

Jimmy fired back. "Well you didn't thank me for mowing the lawn and borrowing sixty chairs from neighbors and buying the wine and beer!" Their fight tainted the party for them, and in retrospect, Jane wished she hadn't looked for kudos from her husband. So many guests had thanked her for a wonderful time. That should have been enough.

Demanding or expecting applause puts you in the position of scorekeeper—"Look what I did, what did you do?"—which is not good for any marriage. Your husband does many things that you don't do—doesn't he take the car to be serviced, balance the checkbook, pay the bills, and take out the garbage? Do you thank him each and every time? We doubt it. A marriage is like any other relationship. You do things, he does other things. It all evens out.

Rule #34: —————————————————————

Don't Nag

Men don't like to be told what to do. So if you don't want your husband to dread coming home or avoid taking your calls at work, or walk out of whatever room you're in, don't nag him. Nagging reminds him of his mother—"Clean your room," "Don't drive so fast," "You're forty, when are you going to get married and give me grandchildren?" Nagging is not only annoying to men, but rarely works. Most men do what they want when they want anyway.

Penny is a typical housewife—a professional, justified nagger. If something needs to be fixed at home, she will talk about it until it's done or until she has begun to annoy even herself. When the faucet in her kitchen started to leak one day, she called her husband Jack at work and told him to call the plumber immediately. "I can't stand that dripping noise. See if he can fix it tomorrow."

When her husband found out it would cost $100, he

told her it was outrageous and that he had a cousin who could fix it for free, but it might take a week because he was extremely busy. Jack was willing to wait. It was an ego thing. He refused to be ripped off. His wife did not understand that. She thought it was about money. So every day for a week, Penny nagged Jack to call his cousin. After two weeks, her voice got louder and meaner. "Forget your cousin. Just spend the lousy $100 and call the plumber. You've spent $100 on cuff links. I'm in the kitchen all day, you're not. The dripping is driving me crazy!"

The nagging went on for about three weeks until Jack's cousin fixed the faucet one afternoon for free. Jack had made up his mind that he was not going to pay $100 for a plumber and that was that. Penny wasted her time and her breath for nothing, as do most naggers. She could have thrown up her hands and said, "Que sera sera, the faucet will be fixed whenever" and spent less time in the kitchen. Better yet, she could have made Jack feel like the king of his castle by agreeing with him that it was outrageous to pay for the plumber and thus avoided all the quarreling.

Sometimes the issues are more serious. Women nag their husbands to stop smoking or to rewrite their wills or pay their taxes on time to avoid penalties. But their husbands end up doing these things "when they get around to it."

So how do you get your husband to do what you want or get anything done around the house if you don't nag? We have a few suggestions:

1. Ask him *once* and *nicely* to do whatever it is and then never mention it again. If he doesn't do it, just accept it and trust that it will be done in his lifetime. We know some women who give their husbands a deadline—if you don't retile the bathroom floor by January, I'll call a contractor myself. Does this work? It depends on your husband. If he's the type to feel challenged by a deadline, fine. But if he's the type to feel pressured and resentful, skip it. Getting along is more important than tiles.

2. Don't try to embarrass him into doing what you want. Some wives will conveniently mention when friends or family are over that "Charlie was going to mow the lawn but hasn't gotten around to it yet" or "John is giving up smoking for the New Year" just as John lights up a cigarette or "George is going to lose thirty pounds this year" as he bites into his fifth hotdog. This is nagging in public—the worst kind of nagging. It doesn't work and your husband will resent it.

3. Focus on yourself. Ask yourself, what's *really* bothering you? Usually when a woman nags her husband, it's not about the thing itself. She may be frustrated in another area of her life—work isn't going well, her kids won't listen, nothing is going her way. She wants to exert some control somewhere, so she takes it out on her husband in the form of dictating chores. If she can get him to do the chores, she can feel in control of the house at least, so the chore takes on monumental importance. In Penny's case, her world won't feel so chaotic if the faucet is fixed. If you real-

ize that this is what's going on, you won't feel the need to nag so much, you will be able to see that you are displacing frustration here and there because other things are bothering you. Sitting down quietly for twenty minutes to examine what's really going on is a good idea if you find yourself nagging your husband and your children a lot. Try it.

4. Try reverse psychology. Tell your husband you don't care if he does the chore or loses weight, that you're okay either way. The less you care, the more he will want to do it.

5. Pretend you're a single parent. If you've asked your husband to help with the kids and he doesn't, you can ask just *once* more. After that, pretend you're a single parent and do it yourself.

Hopefully we have convinced you that nagging is pretty futile. Why not try *not nagging* and see what happens? Maybe he will notice and surprise you by being more helpful. We can't guarantee that the chores will be done on your timetable, but we can guarantee that you will feel more sane, your husband will appreciate being left alone, and you won't fight (well, at least not about that).

Don't Find Fault with Things You Knew About When You Married Him

He drinks or eats too much. He's an underearner or he's a workaholic and always at the office. He's a big flirt or he shows almost no interest in sex. He spends money like water or he's a miser. He's a slob or a neat-freak. He wants to go out all the time or is antisocial. Maybe he's reckless—drives way too fast or is involved in dangerous sports like riding motorcycles or mountain climbing. Whatever it is, you just can't take it anymore.

When you were dating your husband, it was easy to overlook his defects or bad habits because you wanted him to marry you. Maybe you secretly thought that you could change him or that he would tone down his behavior when he settled down with you. Some married men do, but what if yours doesn't?

If you just bought this book, then we suspect that you've let him know a hundred times that you don't like whatever it is. Surprise, surprise . . . he's still doing it (or not doing it).

You have probably tried every imaginable tactic to change him. Perhaps you have dragged him to marriage counseling hoping that a third party would make him see the light and stop. With or without marriage counseling, you no doubt had dozens of long talks on the subject, probably ruining more than one otherwise romantic evening.

If he's an overeater, maybe you have resorted to hiding the cake and cookies in the laundry hamper. If he's a flirt, maybe you have tried tracking him down, beeping him to see if he's really at the office or calling to check exactly how long he went to lunch. If he's a daredevil, perhaps you've begged him on your birthday or wedding anniversary to promise you that he won't race or bungee jump for the sake of your marriage and children. If he doesn't earn as much as you'd like, maybe you've circled help wanted ads in the newspaper and left it for him on the kitchen table.

If any of these tactics worked, you wouldn't be reading this book. They rarely work long-term and he probably resented your interference and did as he pleased when you weren't looking. What can you do? The first thing is to acknowledge that you married him knowing he was like this. Did you really think that if he drank a bottle of wine every time you went out to dinner that he would suddenly become a teetotaler? Or did you think that when he said he really didn't want kids but would have them if you insisted, that he was going to read them bedtime stories and carve pumpkins on Halloween?

Realize that you accepted him, good and bad, when you married him and take some responsibility for your decision. When you stop playing victim ("look what I have to put up with, woe is me"), you will feel calmer and be able to deal with your problem like an adult. Adults accept life and people as they are. There's an expression, "there are no victims, just volunteers." Remember, you married him!

So the bad news is, there is nothing you can do to change him. Our advice is to leave him alone or leave! Make up your mind.

Just tell yourself that whatever it is, is probably never going to change and just live with it. Easier said than done, of course. But you must train yourself to react differently. Every time you "play God" and try to change him, it not only doesn't work, but it zaps you of serenity and energy that could be used on your life, your career, your kids, and hobbies.

So we suggest that every time you want to control or blow up at him for his behavior, call a "designated buddy," a good friend who knows all about your problem, and vent to her. In your own head, in your own home, your husband's bad habit seems flagrant, the end of the world, larger than life. But when you tell a friend—hopefully, another understanding married woman—you gain perspective and you also realize that every husband has or does *something* that his wife can't stand. You may even be able to laugh about it.

For example, Janet often complained to her friends that her husband Jim's compulsive cleaning bothered her to no end. Every night when he came home from work, before even saying hello to her and the kids, he would walk around the house like a robot looking for things out of place. First he'd straighten up all the towels in the bathrooms, replace the toilet paper and tissues, and empty out the wastepaper baskets. Then he'd fluff up the pillows on the sofas and the beds, put away toys, videos, and books, read the mail, return calls, take out the garbage, brush his teeth, comb his hair, and finally change his clothes—a twenty-minute ritual before sitting down to the family dinner. It drove his wife crazy. She couldn't understand why he couldn't pop his head into the kitchen for a quick hi or kiss before cleaning up or clean up after dinner. She felt slighted that she wasn't the first thing he wanted to see when he came home. She also felt his superorganizing was a reflection on *her* housework—not good enough. She was furious. Weren't the towels straight enough? Why did the toys have to be put away if the kids were still playing with them? She told him how she felt, but he insisted that he preferred straightening up *before* dinner. He said it helped him unwind. She even suggested he see a therapist for OCD (obsessive compulsive disorder), but there was only one problem. *He* didn't think anything was wrong.

Sometimes she wondered how she could have married such a neat-freak, instead of someone less rigid and more relaxed. When she complained to her married friends, they laughed and said Jim could clean their house anytime! She didn't think that was funny, but then she gave his habits some thought and concluded that if this was his worst defect, she was pretty lucky. The fact is, the house was always in tip-top shape, bills were paid on time, everything had its place or was filed somewhere. Besides, she hated housework and was lucky that he liked it.

Janet just had a hard time accepting that his cleaning ritual came first. It hurt her ego. But then she decided to put her ego aside and change her attitude. Instead of fuming and waiting for him to say hello, she made sure she was always busy—on the phone with a friend, reading a magazine in the den, or cooking dinner—so that she didn't care or notice as much. She pretended every night that he was twenty minutes late—not that he was cleaning the house for twenty minutes. It worked! Perhaps you have a pet peeve about your husband that could be solved this easily if you change your way of looking at it.

We are not giving you a magic solution. The problem will still be there when you get off the phone, but you will feel differently about it and not be consumed with his shortcomings. Some married women have found it helpful to make a list of all their husband's good qualities when they are burned up about a really bad one, but we doubt you will be able to switch gears that fast. We think it's better to vent and then go about your business. Maybe a day or two later you can think of ten good things about your husband, but don't force it when you're feeling enraged.

More important, try to think of what is going on with you. When you can't accept another person's behavior—particularly your significant other's behavior—it is a clue that something is amiss in your own life. Go inward, look at yourself, rather than try to change him. For example, if you feel your husband could be more ambitious, why not think of ways you could make more money in your job? If you feel your husband could be less controlling, why not start by trying not to control him?

It's best to lead by example. If you want your husband to dress better, dress better yourself. Women who simply complain about their husbands can easily spend the next ten years complaining about them. Is this how you want to live?

We are not asking you to be a doormat, however. If your husband's problem is serious and life-threatening—he gambled away your savings, he drinks so much that he's crashed the car or is involved in illegal activity—we feel it is unacceptable behavior and that you should not put up and shut up. You should give him an ultimatum—change or this marriage is over.

Marcia's marriage reached just that crisis point. When she married her husband, he was a heavy drinker, but over the years, his drinking progressed to the point where he lost jobs, got DWIs, and was in and out of rehabs. After complaining for years, she gave him an ultimatum and he finally joined Alcoholics Anonymous and stopped drinking for good. She was, of course, happy and relieved. However, his addiction to alcohol was replaced by an addiction to the program, not to mention coffee, donuts, and cigarettes. He went to twelve meetings a week, sponsored seven newcomers, and was constantly involved in service work and weekend retreats, and gained a good forty pounds. She felt almost as neglected as when he was drinking. At first she complained about him switching compulsions, but with the help of Alanon (a program for the wives of alcoholics), she realized that he had changed, and that she was better off than before. She was able to throw herself into helping other women with the same problem. The moral of the story: even if your husband does improve in one area, he may take up something else that you don't like. Realize that it's always going to be *something!* No one is perfect.

So whatever your problem with your husband, try not complaining about it for a day, then for a week, and then thirty days. He will notice it and be grateful and you will feel better about yourself.

Also, remember when you can't stand something about your husband, however big or small, that there are a hundred single women out there who would gladly take him off your hands. Don't live in a fishbowl! Talk to your single friends about how hard it is to meet a nice guy who comes home every night, remembers your birthday, pays the bills, plays with the kids, and would never leave you.

Rule #36: _____

It's Easier to Stay Married than Get Married

If you are going through a rough period in your marriage—everything bothers you about him and vice versa, you're fighting all the time or not speaking for days—it's easy to think, "I'll divorce him and find someone better."

You start dwelling on all your husband's faults and annoying habits until you can't remember why you married him. You look at him and don't even think he's cute anymore. Basically you build up a good case in your mind so it becomes easy to end it. At the same time, you start fantasizing about the rich, handsome broker or plastic surgeon you will meet at Club Med or the latest singles hot spot. Instead of meeting your married friends at the diner to vent about your husband the way you have for years, you start calling your single friends to go out dancing.

Who hasn't thought or acted like this on a bad day or month? But unless your marriage is hopeless—he's physically or verbally abusive, has been unfaithful, or you simply don't love him anymore—you may just be going through "the grass is always greener" syndrome or *x*-year itch. Don't give in to it. Take a deep breath, collect yourself, and wait for it to pass, even if it takes hours or months. Don't be rash. Don't make a lifelong decision in a huff or out of bravado. Instead of thinking about walking on the beach with imaginary husband #2, who is of course perfect, think of hiring divorce lawyers, filing papers, firing off accusations, dividing assets, telling your kids that Daddy is moving out, child custody battles, packing up boxes, splitting up the wedding album, taking out the garbage and doing all the other chores he used to do that you take for granted, bad dances and blind dates and spending New Year's and Valentine's Day alone—you know, all the nonfun stuff. Do you still want to leave him? Are you sure there isn't more good than bad?

We know many women who had high hopes when they decided to dump their husbands. They were positive that they would meet someone kinder, richer, taller, with nicer parents, who also liked beach houses and yoga. The reality was they didn't meet anyone good for months, sometimes years.

Before you decide to end your marriage because you're having a bad week or year, think twice. Are you sure you and your husband just don't need a good vacation without the kids? Maybe you're both just stressed out. Are you sure you're not running away from issues that may resurface in your next relationship? Are you simply switching seats on the *Titanic*? And isn't there something you can change about yourself to make your marriage better? Before you give up, have you tried everything? There's a saying, "We take ourselves wherever we go." We know one woman who divorced her husband at thirty-five and married someone similar at fifty. She told us that she has some of the same issues with husband #2 that she had with husband #1. "Men are not that different," she told us.

Before you make a snap decision in the middle of a fight, remember that divorce will not only be painful and costly for you and your husband, but hard on your kids. So before you give up on your marriage, think, think, think! Remember why you married him. Force yourself to make a list of some of his good qualities—yes, he has a few! Sometimes simply changing your attitude, not your marriage, is the answer. More often than not, it's easier to stay married than get married!

Rule #37: _____

Go on the Boot Camp Nice Plan for a Week

Have you and your husband been screaming at each other lately? Have you been picking fights or just plain ignoring him? Thinking bad thoughts? Turning him down for sex? Taking him for granted? Being demanding or difficult?

It's easy to get complacent when you are married. It's easy to become selfish, unloving, critical, self-involved, and inconsiderate. Just about every married woman lapses into bad behavior from time to time! The best cure is to put yourself on the Boot Camp Nice Plan for a week. Why wait? Start today!

What is The Boot Camp Nice Plan? You know how you'll put yourself on a seven-day crash diet to make up for the five pounds you gained gorging on your last vacation? Well, the same concept applies here. But instead of changing your diet, you'll be changing your attitude toward your husband! Here are fifteen suggestions for the Boot Camp Nice Plan—maybe you can come up with your own personal favorites. Read them in the morning and stick to them no matter what!

1. When you are about to say something negative or nasty to your husband, such as "You are so insensitive!," count to five and say something surprisingly light and trivial like "I love that tie!" or "Thanks for making coffee this morning." He will be disarmed and pleasantly surprised. You might remember that in *The Rules* we told you to count to five before you said yes to a date so as to catch your breath and not seem too eager. Counting to five is still a good idea. But now that you're married, counting to five will help you bite your tongue so you say something nice to your husband when you want to be mean. Surely you can find one kind thing a day for seven days to say to the man you said "I do" to!

2. Say yes to sex the whole week and agree to both of your favorite requests!

3. If your husband makes a suggestion or criticizes something about you, agree with him and make an effort to work on whatever it is. Failing that, just don't argue. Silence is golden.

4. If your husband makes a mistake, don't point it out. Again, silence. Remember, this is boot camp.

5. Try to wear pretty clothes all week, not the frumpy stuff you normally wear around the house. Buy a thong (even if you think you look ridiculous in it, but he likes it) and wear that. Don't forget to color your roots.

6. Go back to the gym or turn on your exercise video-

tape if you haven't been working out lately. Working out will help you do the nice plan as there is a direct correlation between exercising and not nagging. You will feel better about yourself and be less likely to find fault with him. Needless to say, nagging is not allowed during nice plan week. So whatever it is you need to have done—the retiling job in the kitchen, for example—let it wait just one more week.

7. Give him a backrub.

8. Make his favorite dinner for no reason.

9. Ask him how his day was even if you are overwhelmed with your own life, have a lot going on, and don't have it in you to really listen. Act interested and make eye contact the whole time!

10. Call him at work just to say, "I miss you and love you," not to ask him for anything or complain about anything.

11. Say thank you for the things he does all the time, like take out the garbage and pay the bills, even if you haven't thanked him for either in five or ten years. He'll appreciate it.

12. When talking to your husband, sprinkle your sentences with "hon" and "sweetheart." You are what you speak. The more lovingly you talk, the more loving you and he will feel.

13. It's not just what you say, but how you say it. The tone of your voice should be soft and tender during the nice plan week. No screaming, no sarcasm, no edge.

14. Let him play golf or go to the gym without your complaining about it, even though you have several

things around the house that you would rather have him do like watch the kids, and especially if he's been working long hours and seems stressed. It's important for him to de-stress. He will be nicer to you.

15. You know that overflowing medicine cabinet/linen closet/cosmetics drawer your husband has been after you to clean up? Clean it this week!

Consistency is the key here. Anybody can be nice to their husbands for an hour or two or a day here and there. But being consistently kind, easygoing, and considerate will make the biggest difference in your marriage.

So whenever you feel yourself lapsing into marriage-rule–breaking, put yourself on the Boot Camp Nice Plan for a week. It really works!

Rule #38:

Don't Go Changin' or Try *Too* Hard

Throughout this book we have given you *Rules* on how to make your husband happy and make your marriage work. We believe that working on yourself is the key to a successful marriage, but there are limits. We don't believe in turning yourself into a pretzel or becoming a completely different person to achieve that goal. If you have to try *that* hard, then you married the wrong person.

How exactly do you know when your husband is making reasonable demands—a clean house, dinner, sex—and when he's going to be miserable no matter what you do? The answer is, if he asks for something and the second you give it to him, he asks for something else and then switches a third time, he's going to be miserable no matter what. If you are married to such a malcontent but you love him and you don't want to leave him, you just have to do the best you can and not feel responsible for his unhappiness. There are some men you just can't please—maybe it's genetic or something having to do with their childhood—so concentrate on making yourself happy and don't worry too much about them. Don't think, "If I just do that" or "I know the *next* thing will make him happy." Yes, the next thing will make him happy—for about five minutes.

Perhaps you can relate to the following scenario. Mitchell married Janet, a securities analyst, knowing that she had little interest in making pot roasts or decorating. The fine china and wineglasses they received as wedding gifts stayed in their boxes for the first year of their marriage—she either made something simple or they ate out or ordered in—and Mitchell didn't seem to mind. But by year six, Mitchell started to complain that Janet didn't cook enough.

Janet agreed and started to cook once or twice a week, but no meal was quite right. When she asked how a dish tasted, Mitchell always found fault. "Too salty" or "Too plain. Can't you make a sauce?" Sometimes it wasn't the food, but the paper napkins—too thin, not the right brand—that were wrong. Sometimes it was the fact that the telephone rang in the middle of a meal. "Can't you tell your friends not to call at dinnertime?" he grumbled. Sometimes he complained that she didn't read the newspaper—only self-help books and fashion magazines. How was he supposed to talk to her about politics and current events over dinner?

Anxious to please her husband, Janet skipped going to the gym once a week to take a culinary course. She started reading the newspaper on the way to work. She decorated the dining room and invited friends and family over on the weekends. She tried making some new dishes.

Mitchell seemed happy, but after a month or so he was on to his next gripe. "You look like you've put on a few pounds. Don't you go to the gym anymore? Maybe you're eating too many of your own desserts."

When she started to go to the gym, lost weight, and bought a few new outfits, he became annoyed that she was spending money. "Why do you need more clothes? Don't you have enough? I don't know where your paycheck goes." It was always something with Mitchell. He was perpetually annoyed.

If you feel that whatever you do is not enough, that your husband is always on your case, then stop trying so hard. Try to meet any reasonable demands but if he starts to switch demands, realize that nothing will make him happy. Know that he is insatiable and focus on being happy yourself. Do not wait to be happy until he is happy. He may never be happy.

Marianne knew Nick had an anger problem when she married him. There was no reasoning with him when he was upset. He screamed, cursed, punched pillows, threw things around the house, then blamed her for his outbursts. "Quit nagging me! I told you I'd fix the VCR when I get around to it. I have more important things to do," he'd scream.

She tried everything—speaking softly, being nice, not asking anything of him, writing him notes, making his favorite meal, walking on eggshells, telling her children, "Leave Daddy alone, he's in a bad mood"—but nothing quieted his temper tantrums. Sometimes his anger was business related and had nothing to do with his wife or kids, but he still vented his rage at home. If you are married to someone like Nick, you have to realize that it's not your fault, he would be this way with any woman he married, so don't feel like a failure or blame yourself for not making your husband calm and happy. You can try your best to not get in his way or aggravate him, but that's about it.

We have heard about men who cheated on their wives and when asked why, they had a dozen different reasons. "She stopped cooking dinner." "She let herself go." "She was always working, never around." Don't believe them. A man who wants to cheat will cheat and then find reasons to blame you. Similarly, a man who makes endless demands cannot be satisfied, so do the best you can, stay or leave, but don't make yourself crazy.

Rule #39: _____

Don't Think Marriage Counseling Is the Answer

Some unhappily married women think that marriage counseling is a magic pill that will make their husbands more attentive or more ambitious, stop their cheating/gambling/drinking or being verbally abusive, or whatever it is that they're upset about. We hate to burst their bubble, but marriage counseling will not work unless it's *his* idea to go—and even then it is no panacea!

When a man wants to see a marriage counselor with you, it means he's committed to the relationship. When it's only *your* idea, you really want to go to "fix" things, he may or may not be committed, he may already have a girlfriend, so we have found it is not as effective. If you are the one to suggest it, he will either be vehemently against it and refuse to go at all, or he will say okay, but find excuses not to go—late client meeting, son's Little League game, traffic, whatever. We know many women who have been stood up at therapists' offices. Or he may show up, but be so angry about going that you're sorry you ever suggested it. Rather than help solve your problems, therapy will become yet another bone of contention. So here is our advice: Do not suggest marriage counseling. If he does not think of it himself and see it as a possible solution, it won't work anyway.

Now you might be thinking, as we all have, "Why? Why is it all up to him?" The answer is that, unfortunately, you can't make a man do things your way. For most men, talking things over with a counselor is not the way they want to solve problems, assuming they will even acknowledge that there is a problem. Most men don't even think there's a problem.

But even if your husband is all for it, we are not convinced that marriage counseling is the answer. Sometimes it can add fuel to the fire. We've spoken to women who have attended marriage counseling with their husbands and tell us that all they did for the full hour was talk about what the other was doing wrong. They left the sessions angrier than when they came in—they wouldn't speak to each other in the car on the way home and sometimes for days afterward.

Janice threatened divorce so many times that her husband Bill decided to go to marriage counseling. She complained that he was not helping her with their three kids and was always coming home late and missing family dinners. He forgot their tenth wedding anniversary, and she even suspected he might be having an affair with his secretary. They hadn't had sex in three months. Bill complained that his wife was always too tired to have sex. Janice shot back that she was too tired to have sex because he got home at 10 P.M. and never helped her around the house or with their children. Bill said he didn't have the time or energy to help with homework, was not cheating, and didn't think 10 P.M. was too late to have sex. They just repeated themselves for the whole hour.

The marriage counselor encouraged the couple to vent their angry feelings but also to remember why they married each other. We gave Janice more practical advice: We told her to quit marriage counseling, spend the money on baby-sitters and cleaning help, stop accusing him of cheating if she didn't have concrete evidence, and take naps during the day so she could have sex with her husband at night. We told her to stop demanding that Bill come home earlier and help her, to stop calling him at the office five times a day, and to try backing off a bit. They have stopped arguing ever since she made these changes.

If you are unhappy, we suggest that rather than going to marriage counseling, you go to a therapist by yourself, or find a support group of married women, where you can share your feelings and be understood. It is not always necessary or even productive to drag your husband through the therapeutic process. You might find that some of your anger has nothing to do with your husband or your marriage, but with you, your childhood, your feelings or career frustrations. You may discover that your husband does not have to change for you to feel better about yourself. So think twice before you call a marriage counselor and try to make your husband tag along—see what changes you can make in yourself first.

Rule #40: _____

Realize that Your Marriage Is Over if He Cheats Even Once

It would be nice to believe that a person can have only one drink, one cigarette, one cookie, and one extramarital affair. However, we believe that once a cheater, always a cheater. We are not telling you that you must divorce your husband for one sexual infidelity. We are just saying that even if you decide to stay married to him, your marriage is really over. Even if he never cheats again, how will you know? How can you trust him? That's the problem, you can't. What do we mean by cheating? We mean the sex act specifically. If your husband is involved while married to you, he is cheating. If he's with her, then he's not thinking about you. It is definitely an either/or situation!

We are not talking about lap dancing and all the other wild stuff that goes on at bachelor parties, massage parlors, flirtatious e-mail in romance chat rooms, singles bars, or business lunches with pretty secretaries. All of the above are not great and should raise a big red flag about the state of your marriage—why is he chatting with other

162

women instead of talking to you?—but they are not grounds for divorce—yet. But don't be naive. E-mail can lead to phone calls can lead to phone sex and eventually hotel trysts. It's not like he's up late because he's playing Nintendo or the stock market. He's behaving badly and you should keep an eye on where all of this may be going.

Don't think that the only men who cheat are alcoholics and ex-convicts. Even "good" men—ministers, outstanding businessmen and pillars of their communities, good fathers who never miss a soccer game, good sons who visit the graves of their mothers more than once a year—have been known to cheat and then lie about it. They have even been caught red-handed, with a hotel receipt or a copy of a telephone bill with a woman's number on it thirty-two times, and still say, "I can't recall . . ."

So if you suspect your husband is cheating, don't waste your time asking him more than once. He will deny it until it is his last day on earth. Even women we know who married their college sweetheart/soul mate/best friend told us that when they confronted their husbands with their suspicions, they denied, denied, denied. Don't lower yourself by asking him predictable questions like "How could you do this to me?" Don't beg him to tell you the whole truth. He won't. Either buy a book on cheating, hire a private investigator, or get a copy of his outgoing cell phone bills, credit card statements, and/or check his e-mail and see for yourself.

Once you are convinced your husband has really cheated, not just flirted, you must decide whether to stay with him or not. It has become popular in recent years to "stand by your man," to believe that husbands who stray are sex addicts who can be rehabilitated with twelve-step programs and intensive therapy. It's become trendy to "work things out" and considered rash to "throw the bum out." We are not so sure about that.

Call us rash or old-fashioned, but we believe that your marriage is over if he sexually cheats even once. And that even if you choose to stay with your husband, you will still suffer a great deal of pain and your needs may still not get met.

This will be particularly true if you married for all the right reasons, such as love, friendship, and fidelity. You will feel devastated by his betrayal and divorce may seem like the only option. Of course, all marriages are different. If you believe that "all men cheat anyway" and are able to look the other way, or you want to stay married for appearance's sake, for convenience's sake, for his parents or yours, for financial or political reasons, for the children, for the neighborhood, for his career or your career or for the country club, you can try to do so, but realize that the marriage will be a sham and it will never be the same.

You will not be the same. You will probably go through the well-known stages of shock and disbelief, self-pity, rage, and revenge no matter how hard you try to forgive and forget and move on. You may wonder every time he comes home late if he's with someone else. (You never thought this way before—you hardly recognize yourself!) You may become obsessed with finding evidence, perhaps looking through his coat pockets for credit-card receipts and pieces of paper. You may do telephone searches on your home phone and his cell phone to see who he is calling. You may start calling his secretary to find out how long his lunch hours are.

Even if you said or thought you forgave him, your resentment will come out wherever possible. You will become the master of zingers, reminding him that he was never too tired for sex with so and so or how much money he threw away on escort services. You may seek revenge and become a bitter, punitive person. Hate will replace love. You may refuse to have sex with him, to talk to him, and will make him sleep in another room. Not a good idea.

You may hate yourself and blame yourself and obsess about all the things *you* did wrong that made him want to cheat. All your waking moments may be filled with "If only I hadn't . . ." You probably won't sleep well at night and your daytime will be hell too. Basically, you will be a wreck. Yes, time will heal the hurt, but it will never erase the wound. We are not insisting that you end the marriage—that's up to you. We are merely pointing out that you should not have false expectations of making your marriage work. You must be realistic.

We believe that if you take him back, it is wrong to rub his nose in his indiscretion or expect him to pay for his mistake for the rest of your marriage. Your motto must be forgive and forget and shut up! There is no point in reconciling if your motive is to make his life hell.

In deciding whether to stay with him or not, ask yourself if he seems genuinely repentant. Are you pretty sure that it was a one-time mistake? Is he willing to do whatever he can to make it up to you, is he frantically making appointments to see a couples counselor, more devoted than ever?

Or is he only sorry that he got caught and even blames you for why he had to go outside his marriage? Men who are not worth keeping say things like, "If you were nicer to me, I wouldn't have had to do this" or "If you weren't always too tired for sex." (Even if you did play a part in the failure of your marriage, that is up to you to look at and is certainly no excuse for his behavior. Don't let him tell you otherwise.)

Worse yet, do you suspect that you caught him only this one time but it could have happened before and could happen again? Did he deny that he cheated until you had concrete proof? Think twice before taking back a cheater *and* a liar.

Maybe you will be the lucky one in a million whose husband does a 100 percent turnaround and you are able to work out the problems that led to his infidelity, and your marriage is even stronger for it. We hope that is the case.

But in most instances, even if you stay together, the marriage will never be quite the same. Whatever you decide to do, do not do it alone. Get the support of your friends, family, your rabbi/priest, or therapist. Infidelity is all too common, and you do not have to go through this painful time alone.

Rule #41: _____

Divorce with Dignity

We believe that you should try the suggestions contained in this book for at least a year before you decide to end your marriage. Haste makes waste. Don't call a divorce lawyer until you have given our *Rules for Marriage* a fair chance or unless your husband has retained one.

We have known women who felt completely hopeless about staying married to their husbands, who were convinced that it was all their husbands' fault and that divorce was the only option. But after practicing some of our *Rules for Marriage* for even a few months, they experienced a total turnaround. They found that by being more loving, less critical, and not expecting their husbands to change that their marriages improved dramatically. They found that by not demanding that their husbands "do their part" their spouses automatically responded in kind. They are no longer talking divorce.

But maybe you have read this book cover to cover and, for whatever reason, have decided that you no longer want to make your marriage work. We agree that not every marriage is salvageable. For example, we do not believe in staying in an emotionally or physically abusive relationship no matter how much you love your husband. You should certainly consider divorce for any of the following reasons:

1. Infidelity. If your husband is a serial cheater or has cheated on you even once (see Rule #40: "Realize that Your Marriage Is Over if He Cheats Even Once"), you are in an irreparable relationship. Move on.

2. Alcoholism or drug abuse. This is an unacceptable situation unless your husband is willing to go to Alcoholics Anonymous, rehab, or some drug treatment program. If you accept living with an active alcoholic or drug addict you are putting yourself in emotional and physical (drunk driving) danger. We know many husbands who wouldn't get sober until their wives threatened divorce.

3. Compulsive gambling. We have heard about men who gambled away their homes and cars without telling their wives. Again, unless a man is willing to get help, you should not stay with him. Once he gets help, you can be supportive, but you should not play martyr to active addiction.

4. Rage and physical violence. We don't know what the percentages are, but there are a certain number of men out there who don't drink, don't smoke, don't cheat, who go to work and pay the bills, but are rageful and violent in the privacy of their homes. If your husband is a rage-aholic, if you are afraid for your life or your children's lives, do not stay married to him.

Other reasons to divorce are less tangible. You have grown apart, he is not meeting your needs, you have met someone else, or you simply have fallen out of love. This sometimes happens and unfortunately, you cannot always will yourself to feel differently. If this is the case and you have tried more sex, romantic vacations, counseling to no avail and believe you would be happier alone or with someone else, you should seek a divorce. It is not fair to yourself or your husband to stay in a loveless marriage.

What do we mean by divorce with *dignity?* We mean realizing that the relationship is not working out and just accepting that instead of assigning blame and being punitive. Divorce with dignity means no bad-mouthing your soon-to-be ex to your kids, family, and friends, or anyone else who cares to listen. It means not lashing out at him, "It's all your fault!," every time he calls to talk about the kids or go over finances. Don't hate him for "ruining" your life. (The less contact, the better.)

Don't hate yourself either. Don't think you're a failure or loser or that your marriage was necessarily a mistake, and live a life of regrets. You once loved him and you made what you thought was the right decision at the time, but you're allowed to change your mind—it's not working anymore and you're mature enough to realize that and move on. Getting divorced doesn't have to mean getting down and dirty, taking your husband to the cleaners, or raking him over the coals. Don't go there, it's a bad road! If you divorce with dignity, it will be easier to get on with your life. The more mean-spirited and vengeful you are, the harder it will be to detach from your ex and move on.

Rule #42: ———————————

Date ASAP after Your Divorce

Forget all the books that tell you to take at least a year to find yourself and heal from a divorce. Some books suggest therapy, some suggest spiritual retreats in India, others suggest celibacy and "detoxing" from men.

We suggest just the opposite, *dating,* but not sleeping around. Even if you hear through the grapevine that your ex is having one-night stands every night of the week, you shouldn't. You're still a *Rules* girl and you don't have sex with a man until you are comfortable doing so. But if you've been through a painful divorce, you need to date ASAP. If you don't jump into the dating scene right away you will forget how to and it will become harder later on. You will become like all your other divorced friends who haven't met anyone in ten years because they're so busy going to self-improvement courses and divorce support groups, where they meet more divorced women, but no men. If some of your friends think that dating right away is impulsive or tell you that you are not allowing yourself enough time to "grieve," stop discussing this with them. Only tell women who will support you in moving on quickly.

We certainly believe in giving yourself as much time as you need to heal. Stay in bed and read books with a box of Kleenex and a box of Oreos by your side. You can look at your wedding album and photos from happier times and weep for two days straight. You can call all your girl-friends and tell them "But I still love him" or "I'll never meet another man," as long as you don't call your ex.

But while you are healing, we suggest you go to the next singles dance, join a dating service, or put a personal ad in a magazine. If you are reluctant to do the bar scene or feel uncomfortable putting yourself out there as a newly single person, we suggest you try on-line dating. It's easy—you don't have to dress up or even leave the house to meet men, which is great if you are still feeling low and not exactly in the mood to put on a pretty face or get out of your sweatpants. And if you follow *The Rules* for on-line dating offered in *The Rules II* (post your photo, let men respond to your ad, don't respond to theirs, let them e-mail first. Don't Instant Message them), you will increase your chances of having a *Rules* relationship.

Note: When we wrote the on-line dating chapter four years ago, we were not big fans of the Internet for several reasons—we worried about the safety of e-mailing and meeting total strangers and we did not like the fact that at that time on-line courtships were more about chatting than physical attraction and chemistry. But now that millions of people are meeting this way, it's a viable alternative—as long as you follow *The Rules.* You will feel better about yourself if you have new men in your life calling and e-mailing you for dates right away.

The only way to recover from a man is to find other men—preferably three or four men—to date. There is safety in numbers. The more men you meet, the more men will be calling you, and dating is the best revenge. Nothing will boost your shattered ego more than your phone ringing again with men calling for dates and buying you flowers.

If you have children at home who are not happy about the divorce and don't want you to date, be discreet, but don't stop dating. Give out your work number or get a cell phone so these men don't have to call you at home and possibly upset your children. Your children are important, but you are allowed to have a life! Being divorced should not be a death sentence.

Don't try to find out if your ex is dating other women or snoop on him or ask your kids for information. Don't use your children as pawns. They are suffering enough. Besides, the less you know, the better. If you find out he is hot and heavy with a woman—particularly the same woman he was seeing on the side when you were still married—you will be tempted to call him up and scream "You left me for *her?!*", or call *her* up and yell, "Marriage-breaker!" Don't do it. Blaming her is like blaming the liquor store for your husband's drinking. Take the high road.

Even thinking and talking to your friends about your ex and how he hurt you will only keep him alive in your heart and keep you from moving on with your life. We have found that the amount of energy a newly divorced woman spends thinking about how to either get back her ex or how to hurt him, if channeled positively, could be used to start a business or redecorate a whole house. Tell your friends not to let you talk about him incessantly. He's no longer living in your house, don't let him live in your head.

Also, don't bad-mouth your ex to your children—remember, you married him and there's no reason they should hate him, especially if he was a good father, but became not necessarily a good husband.

If you have to see your ex or your in-laws from time to time—weddings, soccer games, etc.—be cordial. Do not seek revenge or try to "take him to the cleaners." Get a good lawyer to make sure you are not signing anything foolish. But do not become a bitter, vengeful person in the process. Date others so that you fall in love, find happiness, and no longer even want to hurt your ex. As we said earlier, we do not believe in waiting a year for healing to start dating again. You begin to heal when you date. But we do believe in self-examination. At some point, you should sit down quietly and reflect on why your marriage didn't work out—what were your mistakes, what could you have done differently, so that you don't make the same mistakes with the next boyfriend or husband. Again, any introspection should be done *in between* dates, not instead of them.

Rule #43: _____

Rules for Second Marriages

Second marriages can be easier than first marriages, according to the women we interviewed for this chapter, because you are older and wiser, often choose a more compatible mate, and don't want to get divorced again. But second marriages can also be more complicated because you bring baggage from your first marriage and may have to deal with difficult ex-wives and stepkids. According to one research study, two out of three second marriages that involve kids fail. So know that you have your work cut out for you. On the other hand, you don't have to figure it out all by yourself. We asked several women who have been through it all to share their experiences and offer advice.

"My first marriage was all about status, having a big house and kids. It was all about me, me, me," says Jill, a fifty-year-old woman now in her second marriage. "I was selfish and had a bad attitude. I thought, if it doesn't work out, good-bye, I'll find someone else. Women get what they want and then they say 'ugh, I want someone else.' My second marriage is more of a friendship. I have more patience, tolerance, and understanding. My expectations aren't as high." She also doesn't want to be single again—she was alone for thirteen years in between marriages. "You're more humble the second time around. It's painful to go back out there," she says.

Jill offers these ten rules:

1. Try to be the way you were when you got him in the first place. Try to be in a happy mood, and be pleasant to be with.

2. Don't get lazy about sex. Sometimes greet him at the door with high heels, stockings, and nothing else! Do this even if you don't think your body is so great. Men don't care if you're overweight, you do. Men care more about sex than your weight. Watch sex videos with him. Have sex even if you're tired.

3. Watch the mouth! Be careful what you say, you can't retract it.

4. Men like consistency. They don't like neurotic women, manic and crazy. They stray from that. In order for a man to perform well in business, a man needs stability. Help him with this and he'll stick around.

5. Wear long hair if you can, especially if your husband hates short hair. It's all about what your husband wants. Some men like a woman to wear a ponytail because it's cute. If he likes it, give it a try.

6. Don't belittle him. Build him up, no matter what he does for a living. Nurture him. Pay attention to him.

Be his therapist, listen. Men don't feel close to other men, and they will tell you more when you're not demanding and don't judge them. The nicer you are, the more he'll want to come home to you. Behind every successful man is a woman building him up. I have a friend who would kill you in business, but at home her husband is the boss.

7. Apologize immediately.
8. Make a big fuss when he calls you at work. Don't put him on hold or make him wait. Men buy cell phones and beepers for their wives so they can reach them at all times. Be available to him, be flattered he's calling you, not someone else!
9. Even if you're in a fight, put dinner on the table and have sex.
10. If you need a lot of attention yourself, go elsewhere—to outside sources, to a therapist, friends, work, hobbies, etc. You can't get it all from a man. A man isn't going to save you or give you everything.

Other women told us that the hardest part of a second marriage is the baggage that each person brings to the table. "After a divorce, you build up walls. You have to learn to trust again, you have to work on your attitude," one said.

Then there's the issue of ex-wives and stepchildren. How do you deal with extended family? It's natural to feel some rivalry or bitterness toward his ex-wife, especially if she still communicates or they are friends. Feel whatever you feel, but try not to show any jealousy or disrespect toward her or him. Even if he puts down his ex-wife, you should not agree with him, just listen. He will respect you for not taking sides, even his side. Remember, he married her so he must care about her on some level. He can say anything about her, good or bad, but you shouldn't. Be cordial when she calls or visits. Wish her well. Try to have a relationship with her for the sake of the kids. Try to be understanding and show self-control if she is difficult or rude. Obviously, she may be angry because she feels in some way that you have replaced her and/or she is still single or wants him back.

If you have children from your previous marriage, don't force your husband to have a relationship with them. Let it develop on its own and in its own time. Your kids may resent it that you are divorced and have replaced their father with someone else, so you cannot expect them to welcome your new husband with open arms. Do not play social director even if your children and new husband get along. Just don't interfere either way. Hands off!

If you become the stepmother to his children, you must also proceed with caution. Do not tell your husband how to parent his kids. We spoke to one disgruntled step-mother who thought her husband was spoiling his kids with expensive presents every other weekend and wanted to tell him so. We told her not to interfere. It's normal for a father to try to overcompensate materially for putting his kids through the trauma of divorce. Besides, it's his money. Don't force a relationship with his kids or try to replace their mother. "She will always be their mom, so take a backseat. Let them come to you," says one step-mom, Irene. But don't be a doormat either. You need to work with your husband to establish basic rules—home-

177

work, bedtimes, acceptable language—or you will have chaos.

For example, you may need to tell your stepchildren nicely that rudeness is not okay. When he or she says, "You're not my mother, I don't have to listen to you," you can pleasantly say, "You're right. I'm not your mother. But I am your stepmom and when you are here, I'd like to work together to get along." They may say, "Well, I didn't want you. I don't have to." Quietly say, "Well, maybe one day you will, and I'm going to keep trying!"

It is difficult to have an extended family suddenly thrust on you, especially if you have never been a parent before, so don't judge your feelings or performance too harshly. You may resent it that your stepkids aren't your own or how much work is involved. You may hate yourself if they don't like you. All of the above is perfectly normal.

Try not to complain to their father. He will tell them and they will resent you more. Instead, talk to other stepmothers who can understand your feelings and frustrations and offer guidance or join a stepmother support group.

"I was single for eight years in between marriages. I was not used to sharing or being around so many people. Suddenly I have kids and their friends coming over to our house all the time. It got on my nerves in the beginning. But now it's better," said one stepmom, Ann. Her advice? "Give time time."

Listen to What Men Say

We asked a random sampling of men to tell us what they look for in a wife. Here's what they had to say:

George S., science-fiction writer: "A sexual partner with an imagination. I want my mind titillated. The mind is the most erotic part of the body. I want to act out scenes like I'm the detective and I arrest my wife, or we pretend we're strangers and I pick her up at the bus stop. Stuff like that and videotaping sexual positions. An imaginative sex life takes the boredom out of marriage. You can have an affair within your marriage by pretending you're making love to a stranger so you don't have to go outside your marriage. It's a lot of fun. Also, no nagging."

Roy W., accountant: "Pleasant conversation and a lot of sex."

Bill M., talk-show host: "You're talking to someone who doesn't want to get married. But if I did, this is what I would want—to me, women who think it's important to cook and clean have it all wrong. I was with a woman for five years. I never cared if she cooked. We live in an age of restaurants, takeout, and Boston Chicken. The relationship is not going to live or die on cooking and cleaning. If the relationship is a plane, sex is the fuel, and when you run out of fuel, the plane crashes. I would want my wife to devote all her energy into keeping our sex life alive. This is not a joke, I'm deadly serious. Whatever energy she has should be put into working out, wearing wigs, watching sex videos, buying sex toys. It's a full-time job. If I had a wife, she would not have to fight me over a clothes budget or lingerie money. When you've seen all the clothes somebody has, the relationship is over. But you can't have great varied sex without a brain. I can have sex with a blowup doll only once. I wouldn't marry someone who isn't intelligent. A wife is someone you can spend four hours at an airport with. People fight about a million things, but the main thing is they're not having sex."

Rob W., attorney: "My wife must be my best friend. While some people stress the importance of the sexual component of relationships, the time spent in lovemaking is a relatively small part of the time that a couple spends together. For all the time spent together outside the bedroom, open, honest communication must be the foundation of the relationship. A hug within a loving relationship can do in a moment what psychotherapy, after hundreds of hours, can barely approach. When the souls of a man and woman touch within a genuinely loving relationship, it transports them to a completely new level of awareness—a quantum leap to a place that neither could reach alone. My wife would take me there."

Gene P., computer programmer: "I want three things in a wife: physical attraction, someone on my intellectual level, and a lot of personality."

Craig C., executive recruiter: "What attracted me to the only woman I ever proposed to was that she always had a smile on her face and never complained about anything."

Scott F., real-estate developer: "Trust, unconditional love and commitment, and belief in the long-term goals of marriage and family."

Andrew N., painter: "I wanted someone to love me, care for me, surrender herself to me heart and soul without giving up her person. I wanted someone whom I would not be afraid to tell that I am hurt or sad for fear that she would think poorly of me."

Mark M., doctor: "Assuming that the basic chemistry or attraction is present—since without it no relationship can exist—these are the five qualities I would want in a wife:

1. Honesty. I'm not saying she has to be open and frank all the time, but there must be an absence of deception, subterfuge, or chicanery.
2. Intelligence. When I was single, I don't recall ever going out with an unintelligent woman more than once.
3. A modern attitude. I don't want to be involved with someone who reminds me of my mother or grandmother, straitlaced, superstitious, or neurotic.
4. Common interests. Well, these are desirable, but not absolutely essential.
5. Appearance. We must not delude ourselves into

thinking that appearance isn't important, although maybe not as important as it was when we were eighteen.

Your husband is constantly giving you clues as to what he does and doesn't want in a marriage, whether it's more sex (or more kinky sex), more family dinners, or more fun and spontaneity. Are you listening?

More *Rules* from
Happily Married Women

Eileen F., founder of a modeling agency, married f
five years: "He's got to be Tarzan of the Apes. You
tell him what to do. I've never understood wom
want to be equal with men. Men and women
equal. Let him make the major decisions. Feed
Never say no to sex. Don't give him a reas
Look good. If you look like yesterday's m
what's he going to think? Work hard, b
worth wrecking a marriage. Compromis
the early years, I argued a lot. Now I'l
but I won't say it so violently. It gets
years are the hardest!"

Elaine S., housewife and mo
years: "I'm not up when he leave
as soon as I get up to say 'good
that I'm thinking of him. An
look a gift horse in the mo
tled with a gift my husb

be completely different, but I'd rather leave it in a drawer than return it and hurt his feelings. My feeling is if you complain about gifts, they will surely stop coming."

Helen G.-B., editor and author, married forty years: "The most important ingredient of a happy marriage, I think, is to marry a decent person. Sometimes that's hard to tell if you are besotted by sex, money, looks, even by love, but a successful marriage, I feel, has to be predicated on marrying somebody decent. The world is out there handing you a lot of grief; if you are going home to a rat, it's intolerable! I'm not the first to say this but you should try to laugh with your mate. I don't mean telling jokes but just laughing about happenings in your life. Every man and woman have their own experiences to laugh about. My husband likes to arrive at the airport insanely early. He tells me the ticket says to arrive two hours before check-in. Do you believe *everything* you read, I ask. We have been known to open airports when the moon has barely left the sky. I tease him a lot about this."

Marion M., homemaker, married thirty-two years: "Pick your fights. Talk it out, don't let things fester. Try to grow with your husband instead of growing apart. Try to make him happy. For example, my husband wanted me to stay home with my children because his mother worked when he was growing up and was never home for him, so I stayed at home until my kids were thirteen or fourteen and then got part-time jobs in real estate and selling. It's so easy to get a divorce today, but I believe you start over with the same person anyway."

____ F., personal trainer, married twenty years: "I try not to come between him and the things he feels he

needs to do for his family. For example, he calls his mother who lives alone several times a day just to keep her happy and he has loaned money to different family members. None of my business. I try to set aside special times together, mainly Saturday nights, and also healthy time apart for girls' night out and encourage him to have guys' night out."

Stephanie Y., magazine editor, married seventeen years: "Respect each other's privacy. Don't open his mail, e-mail, journal, or calendar without asking first. Don't assume it's okay to read. Remember your husband is an independent person. Intimacy doesn't equal knowing every single thing about him. Find a way to laugh together at least once a day. Take the time to tell each other a silly joke or something funny the kids said. My husband and I both work full-time and we have kids. It's easy to become grim efficiency experts. Humor softens it up a bit. People at work will actually notice this and comment: 'Wow, you're on the phone with your husband and laughing!' Other-wise, you can get caught up in the New York frame of mind and your life becomes a 'to do' list and you forget to pause to make that call to remember you're a wife and somebody loves you. Sometimes I just call and say 'I'm thinking of you.' Another rule is that we always kiss each other hello and good-bye, even if we don't feel like it, even if it's just a token thing. It's like your wedding ring reminding you that you're with each other."

Jean B., attorney, married ten years: "Never go to bed angry. Clear the air before you hit the pillow."

Miriam G., headhunter, married seven years: "Make goals together to keep you close and excited about the future, such as buying a house, planning a vacation, saving money, etc. Make up quickly. Do things the *exact* way he likes it, especially if he is a control freak. Say 'thank you' and 'I love you' a lot. Let him know that you appreciate him. Don't go more than two weeks without having sex. As a career counselor, I want to add that if you're a dual-career couple with kids, I don't think you can both have high-powered jobs five days a week at the same time without your marriage and kids suffering. It's better if one of the spouses works part-time or they can alternate during the course of their marriage. For example, if the wife slows her career down during the early years to raise their children, her husband can support her career if she wants to get an MBA or take a demanding job that requires traveling when the children are older. Trying to pursue fast-track careers at the same time while raising children is just crazy."

Anne A., editor, married five years: "I have two pretty straightforward rules for my marriage. The first is that I never let one of us leave the house without saying 'good-bye' and 'I love you,' even if we've just had a fight. The reason is more superstitious than anything else. A friend of mine told me that her biggest regret was not saying good-bye to her husband one morning because she was mad at him. He died that day in a car accident. The other rule I have is to never argue with my husband in public. I find this a most unattractive trait in other marriages, so I vowed never to do it. Even light bickering can make others around you feel uncomfortable. It also causes people to gossip about you and your husband and/or offer advice, so keep the fighting private."

Enid O., makeup artist, married five years: "Zip the lip. Always compliment him. Listen when he talks. Tell him you love him a lot. If you go to bed angry, at least try to make up as soon as possible the next day."

Helene S., marriage therapist, married four years: "Make your relationship a priority in your life. Too many people neglect their relationship and focus too much on work, the kids, or other interests. Take time regularly to connect to each other in meaningful ways. For example, schedule a 'date night' once a week with the goal being just to enjoy each other's company. In addition, take time each day to have a positive connection with your spouse. Give them a real, heartfelt hug. Tell them you appreciate something they did or said. Look them in the eye and say hello with the intent to really connect for a moment; ask them about their day or how they're doing and really listen for five minutes (that's all it takes!). How can you expect to have a happy, loving marriage if you don't put energy into maintaining and enhancing your relationship?

Learn how to communicate so that you can express your needs and wants and give feedback and criticism in an effective way. Learn how to listen without interrupting or offering advice, so that you can understand your spouse's perspective on things. Lack of communication and listening skills destroys a relationship over time. Resentments build, which leads to increased tension, fighting, or distance. Communicating doesn't mean that you sit around and talk about your feelings all the time. It does mean that you feel like your spouse is someone you can talk to! You should be able to talk to your spouse about what really matters to you, feel that you really know each other, and have a relationship where you feel loved for who you really are."

Jennifer F., headhunter, married two years: "I try to do things that he wants to do even when I don't want to do them, like pumpkin picking or going to see a scary action movie or hockey game that I have no interest in. I try not to nag him about coming home earlier as he works really late every night. I try to be loving and grateful and really nice to his family, even nicer than I am to my own. I rarely say no to sex."

Final Thoughts from
Our *Rules* Facilitator

As a licensed *Rules* facilitator, I am thrilled that *The Rules* has finally been adapted for married women, so that millions of women can follow what I've long known to be the secret to a long and happy marriage.

On a personal level, I myself am a happily married *Rules* girl. I've been married eight years, my husband and I have two beautiful sons, and I've been on a wonderful journey of love since I first began to follow *The Rules* in the early 90s. My husband calls me many times a day to say I love you and to check up on our boys—and believe me, this is no easy task for a busy New York City attorney. When he comes home late at night, I never worry that he's been anywhere but at the office working hard for the family. He in turn respects me for being the wife, mother, and career woman that I am. I trust him 100 percent. We are secure in our love for each other. If we argue or disagree, he always reassures me by saying, "Honey, let's get over this and make up . . . keep the long-term perspective in mind . . . you know we're going to be married for fifty years." Do you want this? Then follow *The Rules for Marriage*!

Life of course is not a fairy tale, or perfect every day. There is stress when you're a dual-career couple and have children, so I always try, to the best of my ability, to be "easy to live with." I try to tell my husband "I love you" every day, compliment him, try to remember to thank him for small favors, let him sleep late on the weekends, make sure he gets to the gym to work out and relax. In other words, I pay attention to all the things that are taught in *The Rules for Marriage.*

Whether it's a good day or a bad day, I feel at peace with my *Rules* marriage. When I hit the pillow at night and when I awake in the morning, I feel blessed for having known about *The Rules,* following them, and passing them on to others. My life is balanced, healthy, and joyous.

Professionally, I have coached hundreds of women in my work as a certified *Rules* facilitator and career counselor. I have observed many women making mistakes in their marriages like competing with their husbands, criticizing them, not paying enough attention to the little things, taking them for granted, etc. I've seen these marriages deteriorate, sometimes even resulting in divorce. Some women have balked at *The Rules* in general or at my suggestions on how to keep their relationships strong. They refuse to do *The Rules* and as a result, they are just not happy! The truth is, like it or not, it is up to women to manage their relationships. If a woman follows *The*

Rules for dating and in her marriage, the man will respond in kind. What a woman puts out, she will get back.

For example, if a woman has a big job and earns lots of money, even more than her husband, it is best for her to be humble and low-key about it. Men have very fragile egos—right, wrong, or indifferent—and the women I have seen who try to throw their weight around because of their paycheck have pushed their husbands away and emasculated them. On the other hand, women who let their husbands feel like the king of the castle have the greatest chance of living happily ever after in the kingdom. All this takes a lot of work, I know, but the payoff is tremendous. My clients' life stories and my own personal story have proved to me over and over again that *The Rules* really do work.

Remember, it's a lot easier to stay married than get remarried, so get to work and follow *The Rules for Marriage*!

Sincerely,
Nancy Friedberg
www.therulesbook.com
M.A. Organizational Psychology
Columbia University

Fifteen Extra Hints

1. Surprise him! In the middle of a really big fight that's going nowhere, stop and say, "Want to forget this and have sex?"
2. Listen to a story or joke you have heard him tell at least twenty times as if it was the first time. Don't tell him you have heard it before or look annoyed.
3. We told you when you were dating not to give a man clippings or any material about his favorite sports team, sitcom, musician, etc., that you think he might be interested in because he will *know* you like him and such intensity can scare a man away. Just the opposite is true when you are married. Clip out anything you know he would like— upcoming concerts, hot stocks, anything sexy—and leave it on his dresser. He will appreciate your thoughtfulness.
4. When he has a habit you find really annoying, try not to mention it to him—he'll appreciate it.

5. When he calls you at work or home, stop typing or cleaning or doing whatever you are doing. Really listening and giving him your undivided attention—no multitasking—will make him feel extra important. (Don't think he can't tell when your mind is elsewhere.)

6. When he tries on a suit from last year that's tight and complains that the dry cleaner shrunk it, agree with him. "We really should find another dry cleaner!" Do not tell him what you really think, which is that he's gained weight.

7. When your husband misplaces his keys or sunglasses or something and accuses *you* of losing it, then finds it and realizes he misplaced it, not you, don't say, "I told you so," or call him a jerk or demand an apology. Just let it go.

8. If you were about to buy your husband a gift for no particular reason (concert tickets or a leather jacket), or do something above and beyond the call of duty, such as entertain his friends—and then he does something mean or annoying before you get around to doing the nice thing, do not change your mind and throw it in his face. Do not say, "You know, I was going to do *x* but you really blew it, so I changed my mind!" If we waited for our husbands to be perfect or deserving to do something nice, we would never do anything.

9. If you call him at work to tell him something unpleasant—you bounced another check or you hit a car and it's going to cost $500 to fix the dent in the trunk—and realize that he's not having a good day

himself, pretend you are calling just to say hi and wait until he comes home to break the news. If he asks, "What's up?, Why did you call?," just say, "Nothing that can't wait until later." Why make his day worse?

10. We told you when you were dating to wait for the man to say "I love you" first. When you are married, you can say it first, say it a lot.

11. Give him a back rub.

12. Let him sleep late on the weekends.

13. Don't tell him he's driving too fast or to ask for directions when he's lost.

14. Don't drag him shopping if he doesn't want to go.

15. Don't ask him if you look fat or pretty. Too much pressure. Give him a break.

Also Available

The Rules: Time-tested Secrets for Capturing the Heart of Mr. Right
The Rules Dating Journal
Rules Note Cards

For more information about *The Rules:*

1. *Rules* newsletter, Website (www.therulesbook.com), and boards
2. Private consultations with authors
3. *Rules* seminars
4. *Rules* audiotapes
5. *Rules* videotapes
6. *Rules* merchandise and more

For more information, please write to us:

The Rules
FDR Station
P.O. Box 6047
New York, NY 10150

Or visit our Website at
www.therulesbook.com

or call

(212) 388-7910